Tribulation: 2008

by:
Tom Kovach

Tribulation: 2008

by: Tom Kovach

1st Edition, Copyright: August 2008, by 1SG Publishing
4th **Edition**, Copyright: February 2009, by 1SG Publishing
ISBN: 978-0-578-01417-3

Note 1: Unless specified otherwise, all Bible references are from the New King James Version of the Holy Bible — copyright 1982, by Thomas Nelson, Inc., Nashville, Tennessee. Used by permission.

Note 2: Unless specified otherwise, all Greek references and explanations are based upon The NAS New Testament Greek Lexicon. And, all Hebrew references and explanations are based upon The NAS Old Testament Hebrew Lexicon. Both are public domain services provided by Crosswalk.com, a division of Lifeway Christian Bookstores.

Cover art by Tom Kovach.
(Background photo courtesy of NASA-JPL.)

For a summary of updates in various editions, see the Afterword.
(**None** of the original Bible analysis has been changed. The updates only underscore the accuracy of the book's original material.)

1SG Publishing
1483 N. Mt. Juliet Rd. Suite 210
Mount Juliet, TN   37122-3315

"Glory to Jesus the Christ!"
"Glory to Him forever!"

(traditional Ukrainian exchange of greetings)

With grateful thanks to my wife Lynn,
who has stood by me through thick and thin.

With abiding love for my daughter, Anna,
and hope for the salvation of her generation.

With faith that I will get to meet many
of this book's readers when we all get to Heaven.

With special thanks to Pastor Mark Biltz
(Messianic Jewish pastor, El Shaddai Ministries),
who did the research on the solar and lunar eclipses
and their connection to the Hebrew feasts of the next Year of Jubilee.

And, with special thanks to the editors
of *Renew America* and of *WorldNetDaily*,
who have given me a voice in the wilderness of cyberspace.

Table of Contents

Introduction 1
Chapter 1: **The meanings of things** 3
Chapter 2: **Out of time** 22
Chapter 3: **Up from the depths** 83
Chapter 4: **Unfinished business** 107
Afterword   (including notes on updated material) 151
About the Author 155

Introduction

This analysis of Scripture and political events has been 33 years in the preparation — ever since this author first read *The Late, Great Planet Earth*, by Hal Lindsey[1]. (The preparation has been more of this writer than of this writing.) With all due respect to Mr. Lindsey and his work, this author believes that there are a few errors in his conclusions over the years. The same is true with some of the conclusions reached by the investigative videojournalism of Alex Jones[2]. In both cases, however, those errors are very few. And, because Mr. Lindsey comes from the political Right, while Mr. Jones comes from the political Left, the fact that so much of their information fits together underscores both the accuracy and the urgency of those points of convergence.

Because of information that has come to public knowledge recently, other pieces of information that have long been known can now be examined from new angles. Those new angles allow the reader to see the integrated whole of the Biblical predictions regarding the end of this age. Merely looking at a few verses, willy-nilly, could produce a number of wrong conclusions. Hal Lindsey was entirely correct to demonstrate that one must compare Scripture with Scripture, and then with historical and scientific facts, in order to reach proper conclusions about Biblical prophecy. Some of those facts, however, did not yet exist at the time that Mr. Lindsey's first book was published.

---

[1] www.HalLindsey.org
[2] www.InfoWars.com

One error of modern readers is to think that what is seen on the surface (whether of history, politics, geology, or even Scripture) is all that there is. For that reason, many miss the importance of the integration of all those factors. In order to be correct, an understanding of prophecy would need to be correct from all angles simultaneously. (A recurring theme of Jesus' ministry was that people would "be made whole". Seeing things in their "wholeness", or integration, is a key goal of this book.) This presentation will compare some existing views of Biblical prophecy, and then show information that disproves those views. In some cases, this information could "rock your world". The reader is thus forewarned.

NOTE: Events are unfolding so quickly that — only a few days after the release of the download version of this book — a second edition needed to be released. This was largely due to the lawsuit filed against presidential candidate Barack Obama. For months, I had told friends that a Hillary Clinton proxy would "deliver the goods" against her rival, Obama, shortly before the Democratic Party convention. The accuracy of my prediction has more to do with her being politically predictable that with any spiritual insight into her campaign.

As the time of The Tribulation unfolds, politics and religion will no doubt become ever more closely linked. The person that claims to be a Christian, while ignoring the political climate, is like the captain of an ocean liner ignoring a large iceberg ahead. Hopefully, this book will inspire people to pay closer attention to both. (see: Ecclesiastes 7:18)

Chapter 1: The meanings of things

"Now learn this parable from the fig tree: When its branch has already become tender *and puts forth leaves*, you know that summer is near. So you also, when you see all these things, know that it is near — at the doors!" (Matthew 24:32-33, emphasis added)

Far too many people read the Bible as though it were a script for a one-hour TV drama, in which all of the clues are easily shown, and all of the answers can be known immediately. Such a view openly defies the angel's announcement to the Prophet Daniel that certain knowledge would be "sealed till the time of the end". (Daniel 12:9) Many modern views of prophecy are based upon non-Biblical views of religion. For example, many "Christian scholars" lay heavy blame upon the Jews[3], and/or upon our Roman Catholic brethren in Christ[4],

---

[3] Notice that, in order to justify their twisting of history and ethnology, the "Christian Identity" movement (which sometimes calls itself "British Israel") tries to claim that Anna the Prophetess (Luke 2:36; the presentation of Jesus in the Temple) was a member of the Parthians (which they claim includes the British Isles) that were "visiting Jerusalem" in the second chapter of Acts. There are two major logical leaps used to justify this Christian Identity claim. First, if Anna was there when Jesus was presented at the Temple (40 days after His birth), but was part of a group that was "visiting Jerusalem" at the time of Pentecost (49 days after His resurrection, which was 33 years after His birth), then that was an awfully long visit. The very next verse (Luke 2:37) shatters that concept, however, by specifying that Anna was 84 years old when Jesus was presented at the Temple. Therefore, it would've been impossible for her to be part of the Parthians visiting Jerusalem after Jesus ascended into Heaven more than 33 years later. A second logical leap is even simpler to debunk. At the time of the Roman conquests, Britain was known as Gaul. In fact, it would be impossible for Parthia to have anything to do with Britain, because Parthia was located in the opposite direction from Israel. (The Parthian Empire was centered in what is now southwestern Iran.

for all the ills of the world. Although the course of human history is littered with the results of human weakness, and organized religion is certainly no exception, the "divisional" view of prophecy openly defies the goal of Jesus in the famous prayer "that they may be one, just as We are one". (John 17:22) It is the goal of this writer to assure strict scrutiny in this presentation, so that nothing based upon Scripture will contradict anything else in Scripture. In these times of urgency, it is important that believers in Jesus work together, seeking "common union" (from which the word "communion" comes), and set aside as many differences as possible. Jesus will make it right soon enough.

Another key error of modern Bible readers is to forget that the Bible is also a book of law. As such, it must be "rightly divided" (see 2nd Timothy 2:15). Not only must Scripture be compared with Scripture,

---

See: www.parthia.com). For more about the "Christian Identity" movement, see: http://www.british-israel.ca/answers.htm

[4] In an attempt to divide Christendom by referring to the Roman Church as the "whore of Babylon", the same Anglophiles make several logical leaps. In their zeal to lay blame upon Catholics, they first forget that the Christians of ancient Rome were among the most heavily persecuted. Were it not for their faithfulness, much of what we now have in Christianity would've been lost in its infancy. (Have some things been lost, distorted, and/or corrupted during the past two millennia? Yes. But, not as much as some wish to claim. And, that was likely much more the result of human weakness than of malevolent design.) Does human weakness excuse all of the errors of the Roman Church (or any other denomination)? No. But, those errors do not alone single out the Roman Church as the "whore of Babylon". This presentation will show that the knowledge of the identity of the "whore of Babylon" is among those things "sealed till the time of the end". The key is in certain scientific facts that have remained unknown until recent years, coupled with political events in those same recent years. Thus, this "unsealing of knowledge" will make sense upon seeing the information presented later herein. For more on this, see: http://www.wayoflife.org/otimothy/tl030003.htm

but also it must be compared with logic, fact, and science. God is not the author of confusion. (1st Corinthians 14:33) Therefore, the points of Biblical prophecy will make perfect sense ... to those for whom those points are intended. For everyone else, it will seem foolish. (see 1st Corinthians 1:18) At the time of the writing of the Book of Job, it seemed foolish to read that God had stretched out the north over empty space, and hung the Earth upon nothing. (Job 26:7) From the land where Job lived, the north included the vast forests and mountain ranges of Central Asia. But, the *arctic* north (of which Job's people likely knew nothing) consists almost entirely of ice that floats above the "empty space" of the ocean depths. That was not scientifically confirmed until the development of submarine travel beneath the polar ice cap. Likewise, it was only since the invention of spacecraft that the second half of Job's observation was scientifically proven. Job's observation was apparently intended as a confirmation for *modern* people, who often mock the Bible as "unscientific". Thus, the Holy Bible is to be read as a book of authoritative law; a book in which everything is *stare decisis*. (Latin for "already decided"; this phrase is used in legal practice to show that a higher authority has already resolved an issue.) Like any book of law, grammar is important. It holds the key to meaning — not only of the current point, but also of related points. Thus, one must use skill and caution when navigating the grammar of the Holy Bible, just as one would when studying the law. John's warning not to change one word was significant.

Terminology is also important. As a general rule, specific items that are named in the Bible represent specific meanings. Likewise, people named in the Bible have a name that reflects something about who they are or what they do. There are so many memorable examples of the meanings of proper names. One example that is often overlooked is the story of Nabal, a man that owned thousands of sheep and goats. (1st Samuel 25:2-42) His name means "fool". Rejecting customary hospitality, Nabal insulted David and his 600 followers during the time when they were hiding in the wilderness from King Saul. In modern terms, that would be like Joe Dirtfarmer picking a fight with an entire battalion of seasoned militiamen. Regarding the meaning of items, one item that will have specific relevance to this study is the leaf. In the Bible, leaves are described as a) producing beauty, b) producing fruit, and c) producing medicine. These three functions were sometimes literal, and sometimes allegorical. Biblical fruit usually means more people for the Kingdom of God. Some of those people need healing. Not every leaf produces fruit, but every leaf is expected to produce something. The leaves of one tree (the tree of life; Revelation 22:2) produce the healing of *nations.*

Also of key importance to proper Bible study is the ability to let go of prejudices — whether regarding people, groups, or even doctrine. If it conflicts with Scripture, then it is wrong ... *period.* In some cases, though, Scripture seems unclear. In those cases (one in particular: the modern, pre-Tribulational view of "The Rapture"), one must take clues from other Biblical events and allegories. If everything else in the Bible points east, then chances are that a westward-looking doctrine is incorrect — even if there is no specific verse or story that declares a certain doctrine to be wrong. Some modern people, however, refuse to see this point of logic, because it makes them feel uncomfortable. The goal of the Bible is comfort in the *next* world, not this one.

If a person bases his theology upon a "get out of jail free card" — such as the modern view of "The Rapture" as pre-Tribulational — then chances are that such a person's theology is wrong. The early Christians risked torture and death for things as simple as praying over their food in public. Biblical prophecy makes it clear that Christians living in the End Times *will* face hardships and tribulation. Compare Matthew 24:9 with Matthew 24:21. People on Earth are put under two different periods of tribulation; the second period is even worse than the first. Matthew 24:8 shows that the persecution of Christians is only "the beginning of sorrows". If all of the Christians are "raptured out of here", then *who* are those saints that suffer? If your answer is that they came to Christ *after* the rapture, keep in mind the example of the Ethiopian eunuch (Acts 8:26-40), who asked the Apostle Philip, "How can I [understand the Scriptures] unless someone guides me?" Who will guide people to Christ if all the Christians are gone?

Some people claim that the Holy Spirit will teach individual people after The Rapture. But, if the body of Christ is the whole of the Christian believers on Earth, and if the Holy Spirit *resides within* those believers, and if all of those believers are snatched away in the event known as The Rapture, then wouldn't the Holy Spirit also leave this physical world when the believers leave? If the reader does not think that the Holy Spirit can be withdrawn, then consider Psalm 51:11. David considered that, even when he was in sin, being away from the presence of God was the worst possible punishment. Indeed, being separated from God *is* Hell, regardless of where Hell is located. Even more directly, though, 2nd Thessalonians 2:7 makes clear that the only thing preventing the rise of The Antichrist is the Holy Spirit; and, that the Holy Spirit will be "taken out of the way" at a certain point in time.

Nowhere in the Bible is an example of a tree that bears fruit after its leaves are stripped. The modern followers of Jesus the Christ need to wake up and stop waiting for their "get out of jail free card". (Instead, we need to be about our Father's business. Jesus did not run away from Roman government, He stood up to it.) To do otherwise — and to expect the Holy Spirit to do our "dirty work" after we are gone — is to be like the fig tree that has leaves, but no fruit. Jesus cursed that tree, so that it never bore fruit again. (Matthew 21:19) Jesus declared Himself to be the "True Vine". If the early disciples and apostles of Jesus (church leaders) were the branches, then we are the leaves. On any plant, the leaves do the work of producing energy. The branches provide the support structure and direction. In the past six decades, there has been an explosive growth in the number of Christians worldwide. The tree has "put forth leaves". Interestingly, this growth has taken place largely in countries with high degrees of persecution. Why would anyone join a group that is being persecuted? Because, when the people around them see that Christians hold onto the truth of Jesus while under persecution, it becomes a very convincing evidence of that truth. Thus, the leaves that were put forth are producing fruit at an increasing rate. Thus, the harvest must be near. Hence, this book.

now we're ready

All of the above background was needed simply to lay the foundations for being able to use this study properly. As has been shown above, Christians are not guaranteed to escape tribulations in this world. Instead, Jesus guarantees that we *will have* tribulations in this world. (John 16:33) Thus, the modern "prosperity Gospel" doctrine openly defies Jesus. If we are guaranteed to have tribulations, and not escape them, then it is wise to prepare for them. But, how can we prepare for those tribulations unless we know what they are? And, how can we prepare for tribulations by giving strength to our persecutors? And, how can we avoid giving them strength if we have not studied who those persecutors will be?

ancient jobs, modern jobs

Jesus condemned certain specific categories of people in His day. Those included the scribes, the Pharisees, the tax collectors, and the moneychangers. In modern times, those would be the news media, the lawyers and public educators[5] (Pharisees were both), rogue bureaucrats, and the bankers. Who causes trouble for Christians nowadays? Right — the same people that caused trouble for Jesus in those days. Now, with that in mind, why would any Christian vote for a leader that comes from one of those jobs? Is it any wonder that Christians are persecuted by our government, when Christians vote to fill our government with people that do the jobs that Jesus rebuked? Is it any wonder that our government persecutes Christians, when

---

[5] See: "Judge orders homeschoolers into government education", by Bob Unruh, WorldNetDaily, 29 Feb 2008, at: http://www.wnd.com/index.php?fa=PAGE.view&pageId=57679 .

Christians vote for a president that thinks the Constitution is merely a "God-d---ed piece of paper"[6]? Is it any wonder that our government persecutes Christians, when Christians rely upon poorly informed "Christian leaders", instead of studying the Scriptures and making decisions *for themselves*? When the ancient Israelites asked for a king, God explained that it would be a bad move. But, when they persisted in that request, He respected their wishes. How can modern Christians expect *not* to be persecuted, when we choose leaders in government — and even in our churches — that have no regard for God or for His Word? (More on that later.)

ancient religion, modern practice

How do we know that modern political leaders — including many that call themselves "Christians", and are supported by "Christian leaders" — have no regard for God? The answer is simple. "You will know them by their fruits." (see Matthew 5:15-20) The Bible contains a long list of sins, but a short list of "abominations". The most frequently mentioned abomination is homosexuality. If an elected leader promotes homosexuality, or supports another elected official that does so, then that elected official is bearing bad fruit. President George W. Bush actively supported the election campaign of Arnold Schwarzenegger for California governor. Now, Gov. Schwarzenegger is actively supporting the teaching of homosexuality as "normal" in California public schools. Both leaders have borne bad fruit.

---

[6] See: "Bush on the Constitution: A 'godd---ed piece of paper'", by Doug Thompson, Capitol Hill Blue, 05 Dec 2005, at: http://www.capitolhillblue.com/artman/publish/article_7779.shtml .

Based upon the past few decades of history, it should not surprise anyone that California is leading the way in that regard. But, it might surprise some people to discover *why*. There is a place in California, north of San Francisco, called the Bohemian Grove[7]. It belongs to a private group called the Bohemian Club[8]. Journalists in San Francisco started the club in 1872. They wanted to promote the "bohemian lifestyle". Although often associated with the rigors of the "starving artist"[9], the slang meaning for "bohemian" also includes homosexuality and promiscuity[10]. The Bohemian Grove is a place with almost mythical influence over domestic and foreign politics. This writer has heard about it since the mid-1990s, but didn't believe that such a place actually existed. In recent years, though, independent researchers from the Left and the Right have penetrated the Bohemian Grove. The things that they revealed, coupled with other information from decades past, prove that the Bohemian Grove is both a location and a phenomenon. Again, the operative question is "why".

During the times of various Bible characters, there were traitors within both "ethnic" Israel and "religious" Israel (for those people that make such distinctions in the first place). The Bible reserves its strongest language, in both the Old and New Testaments, for the priests and prophets that turned many people away from the One True God and toward various false gods. Some of those false gods are mentioned by

---

[7] See the "Bohemian Grove Fact Sheet", published by the Sonoma County Free Press, at: http://www.sonomacountyfreepress.com/bohos/bohofact.html

[8] See "Bohemian Club" at: http://en.wikipedia.org/wiki/Bohemian_Club

[9] See definition of "bohemian" in the Merriam-Webster dictionary.

[10] See "Bohemianism" at: http://en.wikipedia.org/wiki/Bohemianism

name, and some others are described by their characteristics. Are some of those false gods still worshipped by people today? Are some of those worshippers people of influence in politics and business? Are some of our current government policies the result of worshipping "foreign gods"[11]? Could those policies put unwitting citizens onto the "highway to Hell"? Could those people of influence — their policies and actions, and the spiritual warfare surrounding those policies — usher in the final battle between the "children of God" and the "enemies of God"? Have we already passed the Biblical guideposts that mark the distance between here and Armageddon? The answer to all of those questions is an emphatic *yes*!

We have *already been* in the End Times for several years!

A key purpose of this writing is a look to the near future. But, readers cannot look to the future without first understanding where we are and how we got to this point. The fact is that we are already much farther along the timeline of Biblical prophecy than any "mainstream Christian leader" will ever admit. Why won't they admit it? Because, once the bulk of churchgoing Christians realize where we are, they

---

[11] From his "Infowars" series, see the startling Alex Jones video, "Dark Secrets Inside Bohemian Grove". Jones actually penetrated the security, used a small video camera, and recorded the pagan rituals — praying before a 30-foot statue of an owl — conducted by elite members of business and government. A preview of the video can be seen at: http://www.infowars.com/bg_ceremony_clip.htm

In the 34th chapter of Isaiah, there is a description of the complete desolation left in the wake of God's wrath. Verse 14 is translated differently in various versions. The word translated "screech owl" in the King James Version is translated as "night monsters" in several versions. That word is Lillith, which is the name of a Mesopotamian demon. More about her later.

will ask those leaders, "Why did you go along with the things that led us this far?" (See the warning in Amos 6:3) And, deeper-thinking Christians might ask, "If you're more educated in these matters than we are, then you must've seen this coming. So, why are you still leading us in the *same* direction?" More action-oriented Christians might even — gasp! — actually stop giving *money* to certain churches and organizations. That, in turn, might force certain Christian leaders to go out and get a *job* — kinda like Saint Paul (a tentmaker by trade; see Acts 18:3) and the other early Apostles (mostly fishermen), from whom we have drifted so far. Wouldn't that be a shock to certain portions of our society?

Which do *you* choose: church, or The Christ?

It is an unfortunate fact that many modern "Christian" leaders use the power of their "churches" mainly to build up large numbers of congregants, who put money into the collection coffers. It is much easier to teach the "prosperity Gospel" — and thus reap the financial benefits of happy people paying to "have their ears tickled" (see 2nd Timothy 4:3-4) — than it is to teach people that "in this world, you *will* have tribulation" (John 16:33, emphasis added). The problem is that those prosperity preachers are turning people aside to fables, and to the "doctrines of demons" (1st Timothy 4:1, which specifically refers to preaching in "latter times").

So, when faced with false teachings from a church (in fact, many churches), which will *you* choose: the church, or The Christ? This is not merely an End Times question. Jesus asked His immediate followers and disciples, "But who do *you* say that I am?" (Matthew 16:15, emphasis added) If there is a conflict between the teachings of some individual preacher or congregation, versus the teachings of the Word of God, then we are to "obey God rather than men". (Acts 5:29) And, all of the signs of the Word of God (plus many signs from the surrounding world) indicate that we are already in the End Times.

counting backwards

When a discussion of the End Times comes up, people often try to sidetrack the discussion by claiming that no one knows the "day and hour" of Jesus' return (Matthew 24:36, and Mark 13:32). But, those same people overlook the fact that Jesus also taught many "signs and seasons", so that we *would* know when his coming is "near, even at the doors" (Matthew 24:33). So, let's examine the signs of the End Times by counting backwards from an event that the Bible says will happen "*immediately after* the tribulation of those days" (Matthew 24:29, emphasis added; Mark 13:24).

In the above reference, Jesus was talking about the tribulation against the Christians by the enemies of Christ. But, at some point, Jesus returns to call out His servants from this world. That event is often called "The Rapture". In the past fifty to one hundred years, Christians have become enamored with a "pre-Tribulational" view of The Rapture. This "pre-Trib" view is an End Times equivalent of the "prosperity Gospel", because it holds out a false promise that Christians will escape this world without suffering for Christ. More importantly, the "pre-Trib" position defies the warnings and descriptions that Jesus gave about The Tribulation itself. This can be proven by "back-timing"[12] from a known event that occurs immediately after the final tribulation against Christians (other than The Elect, who have the seal of God to protect them during that time).

Jesus said, "Immediately after the tribulation of those days the sun will be darkened, and the moon will not give its light; the stars will fall from heaven, and the powers of the heavens will be shaken." Recently, scientific calculations by the National Aeronautics and Space Administration (NASA) have shown that the one-year period between Spring 2014 and Spring 2015 will — for the first time in *five hundred years*, with only two exceptions — have a "tetrad" of eclipses. The tetrad is a period of four solar eclipses, each one followed by a lunar eclipse, in a one-year span. Not only is the timing of this tetrad significant, but so is that of the three preceding tetrads.

Remember that Jesus gave very specific events, in order, and said that those events would take place "immediately after" the tribulation of those days. Two of those events — the sun being darkened, and the moon not giving its light — are a precise description of the coupling of solar and lunar eclipses. Further, in two separate books of the Bible (Acts 2:20; Revelation 6:12), there is a specific prediction that the moon will "turn to blood" or "become as blood". That "blood moon" follows a solar eclipse. There is a specific type of lunar eclipse that — because of the relative angles between Sun, Earth, and Moon — is

---

[12] This technique is well-known among radio DJs, who use it to make sure that a song will not play into a scheduled break such as the news segment.

called a "blood moon". And, NASA predicts that the upcoming tetrad will consist of four "blood moons" in a single year!

Twice during the 20th Century, there were tetrads of solar and lunar eclipses. The first occurred in 1948, the year of the founding of the modern State of Israel. The second occurred in 1967, the year of the capture of Jerusalem by the Israeli Army. Could those two heavenly events be mere coincidence? Of course not. But, as TV commercials often proclaim, "Wait, there's more!"

The modern State of Israel being "revived" in 1948 is recognized by many Bible scholars as the point at which the allegorical "fig tree" put forth its leaves. Jesus said, "Now learn this parable from the fig tree: When its branch has already become tender and puts forth leaves, you know that summer is near. So you also, when you see all these things, know that it is near — at the doors!" (Matthew 24:32-33)

There is much in that verse. In addition to the allegorical "fig tree", we see a particular mention of the "leaves". We also see that Jesus specified that "summer is near". As we will see later in this book, there are several reasons to believe that The Tribulation will start in the Summer of 2008. We also see that "it" is "near"; but, that means that it is "not yet". The next chapter will expand that point with specific evidence from Scripture and history.

Summer also brings weeds, which interfere with food crops. During the period when the fig tree put forth its leaves, we see that Satan put forth thistles. Those fruits of evil were world-changing in their own ways. Those things include:

- **1948:** The United Nations declared itself to be the sovereign determiner of the propriety of every human action and freedom (Read Article 29, Paragraph 3, of the 1948 UN Universal Declaration of Human Rights[13]) — thus, the UN declared itself to be equal with God;
- **1949:** the Soviet Union successfully tested its own atomic bomb, thus leading the entire world toward a policy of "mutually assured destruction" for the first time ever.
- **1960:** An activist in California, Pat Maginnis, began a movement to legalize abortion. Four years later, she recruited two other women, and they became known as the "Army of Three". Just as the Communists began the labor-union movement as a way to spread Communism[14], this "Army of Three" used union halls as key locations for spreading their pro-abortion message. There is a common thread among Communism, abortion, homosexuality, Left-wing politics, and Islam. That common thread is rebellion against the God of the Bible and His designs for life.[15]

---

[13] http://www.un.org/Overview/rights.html

[14] Remember that the final sentence of the Communist Manifesto is, "Workers of the world, unite!"

[15] In an interesting linguistic note, the organization that Maginnis founded was called the Association to Repeal Abortion Laws (ARAL). It was the precursor to the National Abortion Rights Action League (NARAL). The linguistics comes in the correlation between the name ARAL and Lake Aral, which was the vicinity of the Battle of Talas in AD 751. That was the only known conflict between the Islamic Arab armies and the Chinese armies. The Arabs defeated the Chinese, and learned much new technology from the Chinese prisoners of war. Abortionists have benefited from new technology in the world of media and communication, and are using it to spread their message of vile rebellion against God by killing unborn babies and convincing society to find it "politically correct".

- **1961:** Yuri Gagarin[16] became the first man to travel into outer space. Upon his return to Earth, he proudly said to the Orthodox Christian Patriarch of Moscow, "I have been to your heavens, but I did not see your God." (To his credit, the Patriarch immediately replied, "If you did not seek Him here, then you will not find Him there, either.") Also in 1961, the Soviet Union detonated a three-stage hydrogen bomb nicknamed "Tzar Bomba" (Emperor Bomb). This was the largest explosion in the history of mankind. (And, because of calculations about potential damage, the Soviets had actually *decreased* the size of the bomb from its original design.) The seismic shock from the explosion went around the world three times!

- **1966:** former carnival barker Anton Szandor LaVey founded The Church of Satan in the city of San Francisco[17].

In all of the above cases, three elements are present. One is that the event marks a dramatic turning point in human history. The other is that it demonstrates a complete defiance of God. The third is that God did not immediately respond in wrath. Consider the "parable of the wheat and the weeds[18]", which Jesus taught in Matthew 13:24-30, to explain that God's wrath is sometimes delayed for greater purposes. Consider also 2nd Peter 3:9, "The Lord is not slack concerning His promise, as some count slackness, but is long-suffering toward us, not willing that any should perish but that all should come to repentance." It is not mere coincidence that the very next verse gives us the "one day is as a thousand years" guidance.

---

[16] One of the early Cosmonauts of the former Soviet Union.

[17] More about that city, its earthquakes, and its seven hills, later in this book

[18] In older translations, it is called "the wheat and the tares"; same meaning.

The leaves of the fig tree began to sprout in 1948. The season of figs is now upon us. Figs are among the first fruit[19] to become ripe. The first act in response to sin — when Adam and Eve discovered that they were naked — was to form clothing from fig leaves. God uses the fig leaf as a marking for the beginning of the age of sin. And, as we will see, God is also using the sign of the fig leaf to mark the "beginning of the end" of the age of sin.

Just prior to the use of the fig leaves for covering, Satan spoke in bodily form to Eve. After the fig harvest (The Tribulation) begins, Satan will again speak in bodily form. The first form was that of a serpent. The second form will be that of a man: The Antichrist.

There has been much speculation about the specific identity of The Antichrist. This writer has done some speculation, but not previously in public writings. Over the years, this writer has come to see that there have been many public figures throughout history that *could have become* The Antichrist. Emperor Nero, Stalin, and Hitler are a few examples. But, something has always prevented someone from assuming that nefarious role. That something, in this writer's opinion, has been the presence of the Holy Spirit. After a period of Tribulation, when the Christian believers are taken from this world, <u>and the Holy Spirit also is withdrawn *with* them,</u> *then* it will become possible for The Antichrist to come into power. Thus, there could — even at this late point in history — be *several* potential candidates for the role of The Antichrist. He will be someone that has a lifelong ambition for

---

[19] Although, technically, a fig is not a fruit. It is an edible flower.

political power and for "change". (Of course, his definition of "change" will be from God's order to a state of rebellion against God.) On the surface, the "winning" candidate for the role of Antichrist will seem to have the best interests of others at heart. But, once he has made the decision to join with Satan, that "candidate" will no longer have a choice about the course of his own life. And, those people that make a decision to join with The Antichrist will likewise lose control over their eternal fate.

During the visions that he had in Revelation, John saw things that occurred both in Heaven and on Earth. From a solid reading of the Bible, we learn that time in Heaven is not necessarily counted the same as time on Earth. There is a decompression of time as things (words, messages, commands, events) travel from Heaven to Earth. This is specifically described in the Book of Daniel (10:10-21), wherein an angel is dispatched by God to deliver an answer to Daniel's prayers. But, once he arrives on Earth, the angel is delayed by a fierce battle with a fallen angel (demon) called the Prince of Persia[20]. The battle lasts for 21 days, and the angel is only able to prevail after summoning help from Archangel Michael, the chief prince of all the warrior angels. The first angel specifically came to give Daniel an understanding of the things that would happen in the last days.

So, in order to understand the periods of time described in the Bible, we must understand time itself. This is part of the meaning of things.

---

[20] There is a violent computer game called "Prince of Persia". Computer games are just one way that young people can be steered away from God.

On the surface, that might seem quite basic. But, without that basic understanding of foundational concepts, the deeper truths that were "sealed until the time of the end" would remain out of reach.

Chapter 2: Out of Time

"But, beloved, do not forget this one thing, that with the Lord one day is as a thousand years, and a thousand years as one day" (2nd Peter 3:8)

The Holy Bible has been described as "both timely and timeless", meaning that it simultaneously applies to immediate situations and to eternal truths. Because the Bible covers all of time and eternity, it only makes sense that time in the Bible does not necessarily conform to time as we now measure it on Earth. Nor do people on Earth measure time as they once did. Time, and our understanding thereof, factors into our ability to understand the Bible — especially as it regards the prophecies of the Latter Days that lead to the End Times.

Some people think that the Latter Days and the End Times are the same thing. They are not. There are four distinct periods in Bible prophecy, progressing in order toward the final battle and the return of Jesus. Those periods are: the Latter Days, the End Times, the Tribulation, and the Great Tribulation (also known as The Time of Jacob's Trouble, or the Time of God's Wrath). Each period gets progressively worse for people living on Earth at that time. As each period progresses, there is less room for doubt or error about God's presence, power, and plans. As the things of God become clearer for people to see, the decision to accept or reject God will also be clearer.

The Latter Days could be described as that point in time when the dominos begin to tip toward the final end of the age. This book is based upon showing the reader that we entered the Latter Days long ago, and there is no turning back. In fact, we have now progressed into the seven-year Tribulation (this sentence was updated from future tense to past tense in the 4th Edition).[21] That is the main thrust of this book. All of the details about the measurement of time are mere supporting points.

Unlike The Tribulation — which is specified as seven years, and is divided into two halves — there is no definite time period for the Latter Days. And, because we read in Revelation that the End Times roughly correspond to silence in Heaven "for *about* half an hour", we do not have an exact length of time for the End Times[22]. Rather, the two periods are simply groupings of events along a timeline. The End Times has a definite beginning that leads up to the Tribulation. Some people will recognize it, and some people will not. The beginning of

---

[21] Research and writing of this book began in February of 2008. The electronic manuscript for this book was hacked from this author's computer in late June of 2008, after this author published columns saying that the California wildfires (ignited by lightning on 20 June 2008) were directly related to that state's decision to resume homosexual "marriage". The columns predicted that, if it was indeed the scenario of Revelation 8:5, an earthquake would follow the wildfires. Exactly 49 days after the court decision, on 05 August 2008, an earthquake struck the state capital of Sacramento. Soon after that earthquake, the hacked file reappeared on this author's computer.

[22] Because, after the silence, the seven angels spend an unknown amount of time *preparing* to blow their trumpets. (Revelation 8:1-6) The Tribulation *precursor* event happens when the angel takes fire from the altar of God and throws it to the Earth. But, the actual Tribulation doesn't start until the disasters accompanying the seven trumpets begin to happen. The fire fell from Heaven, starting wildfires in California, on Friday, 20 Jun 2008. That day was significant. A detailed explanation comes later in this book.

The Tribulation will be marked by a specific event[23]. However, some people — including many Christians — will refuse to recognize the open and very specific event that marks the beginning of The Tribulation. Why will they refuse to recognize it? Because they are still seeking their "get out of jail free card". They will assume, quite wrongly, that anyone still on Earth after The Tribulation has begun is "not a true Christian". They will assume (again, wrongly) that the difficulties they face are for *not* being a Christian. Thus, they will punish *themselves* by becoming part of the "great falling away" (2nd Thessalonians 2:3)[24]. Why would any Christian make such a wrong assumption about their spiritual condition? Because they have been fed a steady diet of "prosperity Gospel". Thus, they have come to believe that anyone that is not financially successful must not be a "true believer". When the world openly mocks, rejects, and persecutes Christians, then those prosperity-seeking Christians will assume (wrongly) that they have been "left behind" after The Rapture. Then,

---

[23] For various reasons, including spiritual attacks by forces of The Enemy, release of this book was delayed until *after* the precursor of The Tribulation. See the above footnote for the date and the signaling event. Things that have happened in the short time since then (this footnote is being typed on Fri, 27 Jun 2008) have only confirmed that the calculations of this book are correct.

[24] That great "falling away" was heralded by news reports that quoted a Pew Research Center poll of 35,000 people. (That is about *40 times* the number of people normally polled for an "accurate" political poll. The larger the sample, the more accurate the poll is considered.) The poll said that a majority *of Christians* do *not* believe their religion is the *only* way to salvation! The poll is called the U.S. Religious Landscape Survey. Pew pre-announced release of the survey just before the storm that caused the California wildfires! (Thus, the "falling away" had *already* taken place before that precursor of The Tribulation — precisely as 2nd Thess. 2:3 says.)

because they make that wrong assumption, they will decide to "get in all the fun that they can" during the first half of the Tribulation.[25]

But, their fun will be fairly short-lived at best. The Tribulation is a period of seven years. It is divided into two halves, 3½ years each. The second half, known as the Great Tribulation, is far worse than the first half. The second half will be separated from the first half by a very specific and unmistakable event. Scholars have differed in their views about this throughout the centuries. So, this presentation is only this author's opinion. But, the opinion is based upon many years of study — not only of the Scriptures, but also of events in the worlds of politics, military, economics, and even other religions.

The event that divides the Tribulation from the Great Tribulation is, in this writer's opinion, The Rapture.

There will be no doubt about the occurrence of The Rapture. Right now, according the best surveys available, about one-sixth of the Earth's population call themselves Christians. But, not all of them are *true* believers. Several places in the Holy Bible — but especially the parables that Jesus told about the ten lepers, and the ten virgins — reveal that only ten percent of the world's population will be saved. The rest have chosen this world over the next. (God does not send people to Hell. People will send *themselves* to Hell, which was

---

[25] The fictional "Left Behind" series of novels — the biggest-selling series of novels in the history of mankind — has probably done more to cement the "Pre-Trib Rapture" concept into the minds of Christians than any other thing. How is it that Christians can absorb *doctrinal beliefs* from books that they already know are *fiction*?! (See: 2nd Thessalonians 2:11.)

specifically created "for the Devil and his angels"[26]. This writer was given a vision for how people send themselves to Hell, and it was truly terrifying.) When one-tenth of the world's population is suddenly gone, the rest of the world's population will finally begin to realize that the truths of the Bible are not matters of individual "choice". The Holy Bible is absolutely true, regardless of whether a person chooses to believe that it is true.

When those remaining on Earth realize that the Christians are gone, then they will usher in a true period of Hell on Earth. Not only will the Christians be gone, but also it is likely that the Holy Spirit will be withdrawn. Jesus told his closest disciples, in the upper room after His resurrection, that the Holy Spirit would come to them shortly after Jesus would return to Heaven. So, it makes sense that the Holy Spirit would return to Heaven shortly before Jesus returns to Earth.

Just prior to that, however, God will command the biggest outpouring of His Holy Spirit in the history of mankind. That will occur in the "last days" (Acts 2:17-18). Young and old, rich and poor, men and women will receive dreams and visions. In one more act of infinite mercy, God will reach out to the people of Earth and literally "inspire" them to avoid the Tribulation to come. For those that refuse, there awaits the very thing they long for: a world without God. After the

---

[26] See both Matthew 25:41 and Revelation 12:9. Note that, in the Gospel version, Jesus described that he "saw" (past tense) this event happen. But, in the Revelation version, it is described in the present tense, but in a future setting. This is an example of how the Bible "steps out of time". There is no conflict between the two descriptions, because Jesus was able to see in an eternal perspective. We must learn, or at least attempt, to do likewise.

believers are snatched away, and God withdraws the Holy Spirit, there will be nothing left on Earth except the corruption of unsaved hearts.

It is for that reason that this author believes that The Rapture marks the midpoint of the seven-year period of Tribulation, and thus the dividing line between the Tribulation and the Great Tribulation. In the jargon of those that study Christian eschatology[27], this belief is called the "Mid-Tribulational Rapture". For short, those that adhere to this theory of belief are called "Mid-Tribbers".

The Mid-Trib Theory strikes a balance between no suffering at all for Christians living at the beginning of the Tribulation (because they are snatched away in a "Pre-Tribulational Rapture"), versus a world of total suffering that few could survive and ending in a "Post-Tribulational Rapture". This author believes that "balance" is a key theme of the entire Bible, and that Jesus lived a balanced life as an example to His followers. One verse that exemplifies the balanced approach to a godly life is Psalm 85:10, "Mercy and truth have met together; Righteousness and peace have kissed."[28] God warns that Christians will suffer. But, in His mercy, He does not allow us to suffer so much that we lose our hope[29] in His salvation through Jesus.

Having now defined the language and parameters of this discussion of "time" as it applies to a study of the End Times described in the Bible,

---

[27] the study of End Times prophecy.

[28] This verse is the central foundation of the book *Changes That Heal*, by Christian psychologist Dr. John Cloud. The book emphasizes balanced life.

[29] see Psalms 9:18.

let us now begin the study itself. This author asserts that the Bible is "outside of time". A preacher on the radio once said that, if one looks at time as a line on a piece of paper, then God is the paper. Time cannot exist without God. But, just as the paper would exist even without anything written upon it, so also God exists without regard to time. That is how Jesus could say, in the past tense, that He "saw" Satan cast down from Heaven like lightning[30]. That is also how Jesus was able to tell the Pharisees, "Most assuredly, I say unto you, before Abraham was, I AM[31]" (John 8:58). In that verse, Jesus not only revealed His eternal nature, but also showed that His eternal nature existed because He was truly one with God the Father. Jesus knew that the Pharisees knew that this statement — declaring one's self to be equal with God — was deserving of death for blasphemy, *unless* it was proven to be true. Jesus proved it to be true by fulfilling every prophecy about the Messiah, including the raising of dead people. A few holy prophets raised dead people by the power of God, but only the Son of God could raise Himself.

In Heaven, in the throne room of God, Jesus is depicted in the sixth chapter of Revelation as a Lamb that is worthy to open the seven seals on the scroll that God holds in His hand. The opening of each seal triggers an event on Earth. The events signal the Latter Days, and lead up to the End Times. (By making things slowly and progressively worse on Earth, God is making the choice more and more clear to the

---

[30] Much more about that point later in this book

[31] Much more about the power of the Holy Name of God later in this book.

people on Earth.[32]) So, just what are the events triggered by the seals, and how do they line up with known events on Earth? And, where do we stand on the Bible timeline leading to Jesus' return?

The first seal is opened in Revelation 6:1-2, "Now I saw when the Lamb opened one of the seals; and I heard one of the four living creatures saying with a voice like thunder, 'Come and see.' And I looked, and behold, a white horse. He who sat on it had a bow; and a crown was given to him, and he went out conquering and to conquer." Those familiar with this chapter have heard of the "Four Horsemen" that ride across the Earth to deliver the various punishments from God. The colors of the horses reveal the nature of the punishments. This rider sits upon a white horse. This point is significant.

Sometimes, the Bible is written in "hidden" language. Sometimes, the answers are right in front of us, but we do not see them.[33] Sometimes, the answers are "sealed until the end" (Daniel 12:9). This author finds that the white horse is a case of God using language (which He also created, when he divided the nations at the Tower of Babel) to seal the knowledge until the time of the end. Is there something in our modern language that is known as a "white horse"? Yes: heroin.

Does heroin fit the *entire* description written in the Bible? Yes. Start with the word "behold". That implies a sudden appearance on the

---

[32] Deuteronomy 30:19, "I call heaven and earth as witnesses today against you, that I have set before you life and death, blessing and cursing; therefore choose life, that both you and your descendants may live."

[33] See: Deuteronomy 29:4, Isaiah 44:18, Jeremiah 5:21, Ezekiel 12:2, Mark 18:8, Romans 11:8, and Romans 11:10.

scene. Heroin does not exist in nature, nor is it naturally derived directly from plants. (By contrast, cocaine is naturally derived from the leaves of the coca plant.) Heroin is chemically synthesized, even though it comes from a base that is derived from the seeds of the opium poppy. Heroin came upon the scene suddenly, having been first synthesized by British chemist C. R. Alder Wright[34]. (Wright's formula was not developed. But, 23 years later, chemist Felix Hoffmann of the Bayer Pharmaceutical Company independently synthesized his own version of "acetylated morphine". This formula was given the name "heroin", from the German word *heroisch*, because the new drug made its users feel "heroic".[35]). By the next year, 1898, Bayer had put heroin on the open market.

Language becomes significant at this point. A person that is "heroic" is often viewed as a "conqueror". The Bible specifies that the rider on the white horse went out conquering and to conquer. How many lives have been conquered by heroin? And, how many national economies have been conquered — or, at least, put under siege "to conquer" — by heroin? But, does heroin fit any other points of description?

The horseman was also given a crown. The Bible does not say that God gave him a crown; only that the rider "was given" a crown. This author used to work as a deputy sheriff in a jail. On many of the inmates' bodies was the same tattoo: the face of an Oriental man wearing a special hat. All of the inmates queried about the tattoo gave

---

[34] http://en.wikipedia.org/wiki/Heroin

[35] *ibid*

the same answer, "That's 'King Heroin'." The drug ruled so much of their lives that they marked their bodies to show their allegiance to this "conqueror". There is a shockingly sad story of a woman that committed suicide at the age of 23, rather than spend any more of her life as a subject of King Heroin[36].

The Bible also says that the rider carried a bow. The bow represents the ability to project power over long distances — as compared to the sword, which must be wielded in battle directly by hand. Does heroin project its power over long distances? Oh, yes. Its reach is global. But, there is also the fact that most heroin use is done by hypodermic syringe. If given a direct vision of "King Heroin", the Apostle John would not have had language to describe the function of that device. The closest he might have come would be a bow[37]. And, if that is correct, then King Heroin meets all of the descriptive elements of the rider on the white horse.

And, if that is correct, then the Last Days began in 1898, when Bayer developed heroin as an over-the-counter, "non-addictive" substitute for morphine and cocaine[38].

---

[36] http://www.1timothy4-13.com/files/chr_vik/king.html

[37] Later in this book, we will examine other linguistic limitations that John would've had while trying to describe weapons on a modern battlefield.

[38] Cocaine addiction had become rampant after the introduction of certain "patent medicines" that touted themselves as cures for a wide variety of ailments (some of which those medicines actually *caused*). The first of those "medicines" was a European mixture called Vin Mariani. That was followed shortly in the United States by a mixture called French Coca Wine. After a local law was passed to prohibit sales of alcohol, the American inventor

That is a conclusion that is rarely, if ever, preached in any modern "feel good" church. Most churches still preach that the Last Days and the End Times are somewhere in the future. Some churches preach that we cannot know when the Last Days and/or the End Times begin. Many churches preach that it doesn't matter, because Christians will not be here to experience any of it. But, this author believes that churches are *consciously avoiding* the preparation of their parishioners for the End Times. And, this author asserts that failing to preach End Times messages — for fear of making members feel uncomfortable, and thus reducing the cash flow in collection plates — is the primary failure of modern churches. This author further asserts that such gross neglect might be the primary reason for the verse, "For the love of money is a root of all kinds of evil, for which some have strayed from the faith in their greediness, and pierced themselves through with many sorrows." (1st Timothy 6:10. Some translations say "all evil".)

Another word for a prophet was a "seer". A prophet is one that sees things that God puts in place. Some of those things are invisible to any but the gifted prophet. Other things are there for anyone to see, but remain unseen because of the uncaring attitude of those looking. The Apostle Paul wrote, "Pursue love, and desire spiritual gifts, but especially that you may prophesy." (1st Corinthians 14:1) Anyone can ask the Holy Spirit to open their eyes to the truth, <u>but few will *ask*</u>. For those that do, the Bible becomes a treasure chest of revealed truth. This writer's hope is that all who read this will look up to God the

---

came up with a new, cocaine-based drink called ... Coca-Cola. See: http://en.wikipedia.org/wiki/Coca-Cola

Father (Yehowah), seek salvation through His Son Jesus (Yeshua), and seek truth and wisdom via His Holy Spirit. Then, more people will see the "signs and seasons" that have been available in the Bible for centuries. (But, until heroin was given the nickname "horse", the knowledge had been "sealed until the time of the end". As further proof of this concept, consider that this was the first seal opened[39])

When the second seal of the scroll is opened (Revelation 6:3-4), a rider goes out on a red horse. This rider has the power "to take peace from the earth", that people should kill one another, and he "is given a great sword". Again, the color of the horse is significant. Red[40] is the color of Communism. That philosophy, which is bent on global domination, is responsible for killing more people than any other philosophy or government since the ancient Roman Empire. And, the death toll from Communism surpassed that of Rome decades ago.

Further, the agents of Communism have "taken peace from the earth" by not only dominating the citizens of their own countries, and attacking the citizens of neighboring countries, but also by selling death through espionage and terrorism. Communist countries such as China and the former Soviet Union were known for using proxies and "satellite countries" to do their dirty work. But, is there more?

---

[39] When the angel tells Daniel to "seal the book until the time of the end", that is the last mention of a seal in the Old Testament. There are several mentions of a seal in the New Testament, but they are seals upon the soul and body. The first mention of opening the seal of a book (scroll) is in Revelation. There is no seal opened in the Bible from the end of Daniel until the sixth chapter of Revelation, when the rider goes out on a white horse.

The Bible specifies that the rider on the red horse "is given" a great sword. The most destructive weapon in the history of mankind is the nuclear bomb. The United States developed atomic power. Released documents, formerly Top Secret, show that the Manhattan Project was created partly because American scientists and military intelligence discovered that the Nazi government of Germany was working to harness atomic power. America needed to beat Germany to that discovery, so that the Nazis could not threaten the world with annihilation. And, history shows that America won the race. We developed the atomic reactor; and, later, an atomic bomb.

By contrast, the Soviet Union *acquired* their atomic bomb technology because it "was given" to them by the treason of Julius and Ethel Rosenberg. Thus, the country that first implemented a Communist (Red) government also "was given" the greatest sword of history. Thus, the rider on the red horse is Communism, which took over the Russian Empire in 1917.

In an interesting historical note, at the time of the Bolshevik Revolution, Russia was the last *Christian* empire on Earth. Moscow had earned the title of the "Third Rome" — having become the repository of Christian thought after the pagan Huns had sacked Rome in AD 451, and the Muslim Turks had sacked Constantinople in AD 1453. Thus, it was no accident that the Communist philosophy of Karl Marx, who was a German, came to be implemented first in Russia. Communism is an attack upon Christianity. It veils itself as an attempt to have "Christianity

---

[40] In the Old Testament, one group of people that continually trouble the Israelites is the Edomites. Their name means "red people".

without Christ", which is impossible. Even after more than 70 years of Communist domination, though, the Russian people still used their traditional name, *Vosskressenie*, for Sunday. The Russian *Vosskressenie* translates to "Resurrection Day". (So ... why do we call it "Sun" Day here in "Christian" America? The Mesopotamian sun god is Baal. Hmmm.)

The third seal is opened in Revelation 6:5-6. A rider on a black horse appears. The rider holds a pair of balance-scales[41] in his hand. John then hears a voice saying, "A quart of wheat for a denarius, and three quarts of barley for a denarius; and do not harm the oil and the wine." Most people presume that the horse and rider symbolize famine; and, that is one possibility. But, the focus seems to be on the *price* of the grains, and not upon the scarcity of the grains. (Although, the price could be caused by scarcity. But, could there be another cause?)

During the 1930s, two events converged. Those two events combined to create a long-lasting effect upon food production and the world economy. So, although the rider on the black horse *could* symbolize the famine in Post-World-War-One Germany, which led to hyperinflation in that country, it is also possible that the rider on the black horse symbolizes the Dust Bowl and the Great Depression in the United States. Either of those combined events (or both) fit the description of the rider on the black horse.

The color black not only symbolizes famine and scarcity, it can also symbolize secrecy. Many financial scholars claim that the Great

---

[41] As distinguished from any other type of scales, because the Greek word is *zugos*, from the root word meaning "yoke". Interestingly, this type of scale can be manipulated.

Depression was a manufactured event.[42] Regardless of whether it was created by design, the fact remains that the Great Depression ushered in a time of far greater control by the Federal government. This was true both in the United States under President Franklin D. Roosevelt, and in Nazi Germany under Chancellor Adolf Hitler.

The effect in the United States was a shift from government responding to the economy to a government *controlling* the economy. It also brought a shift from people relying upon themselves — with a dual safety network of family and church — to a society that relies upon government for their sustenance in both good times and bad. In other words, government became the provider of daily bread. Thus, the government set itself up as a god.

Regardless of whether the rider on the black horse symbolizes a specific national event, or a group of similar events in various nations (keep in mind that Stalin was engineering the Ukrainian potato famine, and Germany's food supply was spoiling due to hyperinflation of money, during that same time), the bottom line remains that a global societal shift in focus (away from God) occurred when the third seal was opened.

The fourth seal is opened in Revelation 6:7-8. The rider is on a pale horse (some translations say "gray" or "ashen"[43]). The name of the

---

[42] Thus, the double meaning of the "balance scale" fits with the scenario that the Great Depression could have been artificially created in order to usher in an era of inflation, which only benefits those at the very top of the economic system. The temptation to manipulate the economy is even stronger during times of sudden necessity, as shown by price hikes accompanying hurricanes.

[43] Note that the ashes from the furnaces of the Nazi death camps fell upon the surrounding villages.

rider is Death, and he is followed by Hades (the Greek word for the realm of the dead, or for the entire population of that realm). Power was given to them over a fourth of the earth, "to kill with sword, with hunger, with death[44], and by the beasts of the earth."

An interesting point here is the idea that some people are killed "with death". The Greek word used here is *Thanatos*[45], which means the misery of separating soul from body. That normally happens in death. But, is there another time when soul can be separated from body? (The Greek word used for "kill" is the word *apokteino*, which refers mainly to physical death, while *Thanatos* refers to spiritual death.)

During the 1930s and 1940s, three major systems of captivity and deadly misery were created on large scales. The most famous was the concentration camps of Nazi Germany. Their allies in the Japanese

---

[44] From the New King James Version. Some other versions say "pestilence". Based upon the Greek word in the original, this author believes that "death" is the more correct translation, as explained in Footnote Number 45.

In order to remain true to the meaning of the Greek word, any "pestilence" would need to be a slowly debilitating one, such as cancer or tuberculosis. An epidemic of TB is so feared in the medical community that, as far back as 19 July 1884, President Chester Arthur issued an executive order that all potential immigrants to the United States be quarantined for testing before being admitted beyond their port of entry. The United States remains vigilant against TB; but, illegal aliens carry diseases into the country by avoiding the testing procedures. The US prison population, which has four times the proportion of illegal aliens as the general population, is on the verge of a TB epidemic. (And, eventually, people get out of prison....)

[45] In a resurrection worship hymn of the Greek Orthodox Church, it is sung that Jesus trampled Death by means of *Thanatos*. Although it is translated in English as He "trampled down Death by death", it actually means more. It means that Jesus defeated Death by willingly suffering separation from not only His earthly physical body, but also separation from God the Father. The condition of being separated from God *is* Hell, regardless of time or location.

Empire did the same thing, but sometimes in a slightly different way. Both used their captured enemies to do hard labor, which often benefited the war efforts; but, the Japanese tended to use many smaller camps, instead of a few large camps. Also, the Japanese used forced labor imported from conquered nations, especially Korea[46]. Simultaneously, the Soviet Union instituted its systems of "strawberry fields" and gulags. (The Beatles sang a song praising Communism, by extolling "Strawberry Fields[47] Forever".) Some of those captives were singled out for being Jewish, but others were taken captive for resisting tyranny. Thus, we see that, before and during World War Two, various totalitarian regimes took over approximately one-fourth of the Earth, and killed people "with death", as well as by the other means listed in the passage.

Those means included "the beasts of the earth". But, how can a government kill people by means of animals? Or, was there another meaning for the term "beasts of the earth"? My column, "The beasts of the earth[48]", addresses this topic. The Greek word used, *therion*,

---

[46] To this day, in Korea, there is evidence of the rape of the Korean forests by clear-cutting under Japanese occupation, which started in 1911. There was at least as much damage to the overall Korean countryside by the land-rape as there was by the artillery fire of the Korean War that followed World War 2.

[47] Stalin would use his "useful idiots" to implement change in Russia by means of their treason. Then, to make sure that those people never told anyone how they had been used, Stalin had them taken to remote areas and hosed down by machinegun fire. So much blood ran in the mass killings that Stalin referred to the areas as his "strawberry fields". That a musical group would proclaim such a thing should go on forever is a testimony to the true nature of The Beatles and their messages of anti-God and pro-revolution.

[48] http://www.renewamerica.us/columns/kovach/070705

can mean either a wild animal or "a brutish, bestial man"[49]. Genetic experiments upon humans under Hitler became well known shortly after the Allies liberated the Nazi death camps. But, only in recent years has it become known that Stalin, as early as 1925, was already trying to field genetically-engineered soldiers from "humanzee[50]" stock. Those soldiers were meant to be impervious to pain, hunger, and moral thoughts. It is unclear if any were ever actually used in battle. But, the fact that any government leader would even try to produce such a "trans-human" shows a complete disrespect for the laws and ways of God. It is an escalation of the separation from God that characterizes the Latter Days leading up to the End Times.

The first four seals of Revelation 6 deal with real events in the physical world. The fifth seal is opened in verses 9-11, and deals with events in the both the physical and the spiritual worlds. The first four seals were described in two verses each, but the fifth seal is described in three verses. The first four seals initiate an immediate (in Bible time) action, but the fifth seal reveals that a certain amount of patience will be required to see this action to completion.

The event that takes time for completion is the killing of a specific number of Christian believers, who are killed "... because of the word of God and because of the testimony which they had maintained." The

---

[49] from The NAS New Testament Greek Lexicon, at: www.crosswalk.com

[50] An actual mix, via artificial insemination, of human and chimpanzee. In recent years, this type of experimentation has been revived in Great Britain. It has become the topic of intense debate in Parliament. But, legal loopholes (probably put there by design) currently allow the experiments to continue.

number required is not revealed. That number is apparently known only to God. But, at the time that the fifth seal is opened, it will only take "a little while" for that number to be completed.

After the end of World War Two, a revolution put the Communists in charge of the government of China. Shortly after that, the Chinese Communists began a series of purges that ushered in the largest number of Christians killed by a single regime in the history of mankind. Various advocacy groups[51] have estimated that more Christians were killed in the 20th Century than in all the preceding centuries of the Christian era combined. Add to this the number of unborn babies — who have not yet committed any act of sin[52] — killed by abortion, and the reader can see how a righteous God could be angered to the point of wrathful destruction of Earth and all of its inhabitants! And, apparently, that's what most people seek.

As if people seeking destruction by God is not bizarre enough, some people seem intent on seeking the destruction of the world by man-made devices. The sixth seal is opened in Revelation 6:12-16. This is the longest number of verses so far to describe events initiated by the opening of the seals on the scroll in the hand of God. Before going on, let's recap the events associated with the opening of the seals so far.

The first seal was opened (in Earth time) in 1898, when the newly-created heroin became a commercial product that "went out conquering and to conquer". (That was also the year of the Spanish-

---

[51] such as Voice of the Martyrs, and the Persecuted Church Collection

[52] Much more about that point, later in this book.

American War. More on that later. It was also the year that activist Theodor Hertzel founded the modern Zionist movement.) The second seal was opened in 1917, when Communism toppled the last Christian empire. The third was opened in 1929, the year of the start of the Great Depression. (And, the subsequent famines in the United States, Germany, and the USSR led to a huge increase in central government power in all three countries.[53]) The opening of the fourth seal could've been at any time within a span of about 12 years. But, this author believes that it is tied to a specific event, *Kristallnacht*[54], which marked the formal beginning of the roundup of Jews by the Nazi government. (Nazi concentration camps already existed, and the Jews had already been confined to their traditional ghettos, but the actual roundup of Jews did not begin until that specific event.) *Kristallnacht*

---

[53] Franklin D. Roosevelt and Adolph Hitler came to power <u>within ten days of each other</u> in January of 1933. That same year, Stalin began using forced "labor camps" as part of his five-year plans of national industrialization.

For more about the Communist nature of FDR's sweeping reform programs, see my column, "Minimum wage: New Deal vs. Square Deal", 30 Aug 2005, at: http://www.renewamerica.us/columns/kovach/050830

[54] Literally, German for "the night of broken glass". It is also sometimes called the "night of the long knives", for the bayonets used by the SS troops.

It is important to note that <u>Hitler also ordered the roundups of specific Christian groups</u>. Russian Orthodox Christians, for example, were known for relying upon their faith and traditions to resist Communism. Polish Catholic Christians were known for resisting the Nazis by hiding Jews within homes, businesses, churches, and convents. Jehovah's Witnesses*, although German citizens, refused to serve in their county's military. They were put into concentration camps, forced to wear purple triangles on their clothing, and then given the option of recanting their faith or being put to death. The vast majority chose death over the Nazi regime. Nazism is anti-God to its core. (*Jehovah's Witnesses are not Christian, but are thought of by non-believers to be a Christian group.)

occurred on Wednesday[55], 09 November 1938. The fifth seal was opened in 1948, when the Communist Chinese began the largest purge of Christians in the history of mankind. (So, for those that might claim that the fourth seal "belongs" to the Jews by way of persecution, the fifth seal definitely "belongs" to the Christians by way of persecution.) Also, in 1948 the modern State of Israel was born.

The sixth seal returns to events in the physical world[56]. This is the longest and most detailed description (verses 12-17) of any seal except the seventh. In order for an event in the physical world to qualify as corresponding to the opening of the sixth seal, it would need to match all of the details written. Has such an event occurred; and, did that event occur in correct chronological order after the other five seals?

The United States detonated the first hydrogen bomb, nicknamed Ivy Mike, at Enewetak Atoll in the Pacific Ocean on 01 November 1952. This event marks the graduation from the atomic bomb[57] (such as those used against Hiroshima and Nagasaki) to the thermonuclear bomb category, with hundreds of times more destructive power. How does the description of this event line up with the description of the sixth seal of Revelation?

---

[55] On any Wednesday evening, many Christians would've been gathered together, singing in churches. Thus, they would've been less likely to hear the noises of the roundup than on other nights of the week.

[56] Although, in *all* cases, events in the physical world are triggered by events in the spiritual world. The opening of the seals is simply the most graphic example of that fact.

[57] Interestingly, the nickname for the original atomic bomb test program was "Trinity". The test detonation site is now a National Historic Landmark.

The beginning of the description (verse 12) follows, in precise sequence, a basic description of a thermonuclear explosion. The explosion of Ivy Mike caused a violent earthquake, and created a crater more than a mile in diameter. The crater was deeper than the Houston Astrodome is tall, and completely destroyed the island on which the bomb had been placed.[58]

Verse 12 goes into specific detail, though, by saying that "the sun became black as sackcloth made of hair, and the whole moon became like blood." Under normal circumstances, this would imply both a solar and a lunar eclipse. But, a thermonuclear detonation is not a normal circumstance. And, as covered elsewhere in this book, God uses a combination of solar and lunar eclipses to mark other events.

Certain things happen in rapid succession in such an explosion. One is an intense ball of light and fire. Some scientists note that this type of nuclear explosion momentarily produces a temperature hotter than the surface of the sun. As the heat and blast rapidly move outward in a shock wave, it actually *bakes* the air in front of it. As the blast and heat energies ventilate upward, the shock wave produces a vacuum behind itself. That vacuum literally sucks the dirt from the ground.

It is the dust from the ground that produces the stem of the famous mushroom-shaped cloud that is the signature of a thermonuclear explosion. Dust is thrown 15 to 20 miles into the sky in a matter of a few seconds! Among other things, that cloud of dust momentarily

---

[58] To compare "before" and "after" photographs, see:
http://en.wikipedia.org/wiki/Ivy_Mike

blocks the sun ... if the blast is in the daytime. The blast of Operation Ivy Mike was in the daytime. So much earth was dislodged in the blast that it actually wiped out the entire island upon which the bomb had been placed.

Dust from nuclear blast blocks the sun.
Light below cloud is from *fireball*, not sun.
(US Government photo: "Harry 1" blast at the Nevada Test Range, 19 May 1953)

Regardless of whether the blast is in day or night, the high-altitude dust cloud will linger in the upper atmosphere for days. During that time, moonlight is filtered through the dust — just as it is after a volcanic eruption. In both cases, the moon takes on a reddish color. Thus, even *without* a solar or lunar eclipse, the sun was darkened and the moon "became as blood".

In Verse 13, the next part of the description of the event that follows the opening of the sixth seal says that "the stars of the sky fell to earth, as a fig tree casts its unripe figs when shaken by a great wind". On the surface, this part of the description would not seem to fit, because this blast occurred in the daytime. But, when one views the details of a thermonuclear explosion, one can see that the Apostle John — who had no precise language for describing such a blast — could easily have presumed that the stars had been shaken from the sky.

Fig-shaped fireballs spew from *bottom* of blast cloud as it rises.
To the Apostle John, it would look like stars shaken from the sky.
Note the clouds in the sky "rolled back like a scroll", also.
(US Government photo: "Ivy King" blast, 16 Nov 1952)

As the photo on the previous page shows, balls of fire spew in all directions from the bottom of the nuclear blast cloud as it rises toward the edge of outer space. John's analogy of figs and a great wind is also fitting. The balls of fire spewing from the bottom of the rising mushroom cloud, in addition to glowing like stars, are also shaped like figs. (We will examine the analogy of the fig tree in more detail later.)

The thermonuclear blast is accompanied by two enormous blasts of wind. The first is the blast shock wave going *outward from* the detonation site. The second is the "Return wave" — a huge rush of air *inward toward* the detonation site — to fill the vacuum created by the original blast shock wave. The mushroom cloud could also be said to be tree-shaped. Thus, "stars" fell from the sky like figs from a tree shaken by a great wind. How else could John have described it?

As the photo also shows, consistent with the continuing description in Verse 14, the sky was "split apart like a scroll when it is rolled up". That is a precise depiction of the "condensation cloud" that is produced inside the "rarefaction zone" (where the heat bakes the air) behind the "shock front" of the blast effect. The shock wave moves so fast that, as the superheated air cools off behind the "shock front", the cooling air forms a cloud. The cloud ring parallels the shock wave, which moves simultaneously outward and upward from the blast. If watched from the ground-up perspective (as it appears that John's vision did), then the vacuum that the blast produces ahead of the condensation cloud would actually discolor the sky (because the refraction of sunlight through the air gives the sky its blue color). Thus, it would appear as though the sky had been "split open" — because it actually *had been* split open! There was no way that a fisherman living 2,000 years ago could have imagined a donut-shaped cloud ring, moving at supersonic speed, and rolling up just like a scroll across the sky. The only way that he could have described a thermonuclear blast so accurately is if it had truly been a vision from God. But, wait, there's more.

Verse 14 continues by saying that "every mountain and island were moved out of their places". Three days after the Ivy Mike blast, the most powerful earthquakes ever recorded by a seismograph occurred on the Kamchatka Peninsula off the eastern coast of Siberia. The first quake measured 9.0 on the Richter scale, with strong aftershocks. A look at the tectonic plates of the Earth's crust shows that the Enewetak Atoll is almost dead center in the Pacific Plate. Along the east coast of Asia, the plate mostly parallels the curvature of the Chinese coastline. But, there is a point between the Asian curve of the plate and the Alaskan curve of the plate. The Alaskan curve mostly parallels the Aleutian Island chain. The two curves come together in a point, which is pointed almost dead center toward the Kamchatka Peninsula. Thus, any seismic shock wave from the center of the Pacific Plate would have been concentrated — like an echo between two stone cliffs — at the point where the two curves come together. Thus, the seismic wave was intensified to create the strongest earthquake on record. (Could this blast — and other test blasts like it — have disrupted Earth's crust so much that a never-ending series of earthquakes was created? The record of earthquakes seems to suggest that possibility).

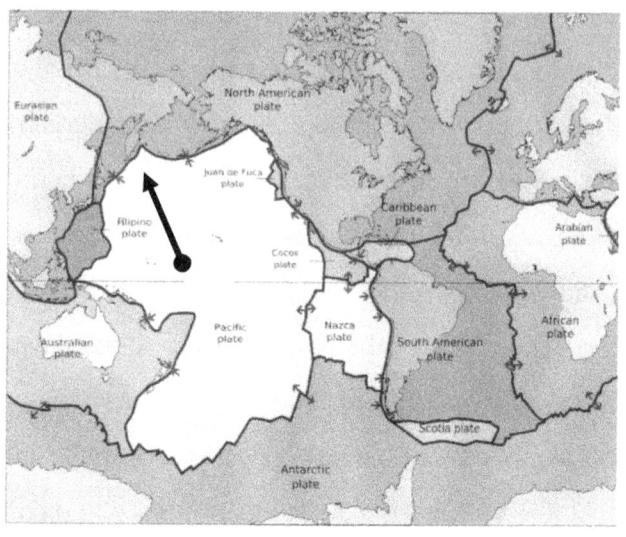

Blast came from center of Pacific Plate to point at Kamchatka.
Seismic energy was funneled into largest-ever-recorded earthquake.
(Map source: Wikipedia[59].)

Verse 14 continues by saying, "... every mountain and island were moved out of their places." This writer was not able to find specific seismic data related to the Ivy Mike explosion. However, some data was available for other explosions, including the Soviet Union's test of the largest man-made explosion in history: Tzar Bomba in 1961. The seismic shock wave from Tzar Bomba was recorded to have gone around the entire Earth *three* times! Notably, that explosion was about three times larger than Ivy Mike. Thus, one can infer that the seismic wave from Ivy Mike went around the entire Earth at least once. Thus, "every mountain and island" was moved from its place, even if that movement was only a millimeter or two.

---

[59] For detailed info, see: http://en.wikipedia.org/wiki/Pacific_Plate

In other places around the globe, the seismic energy might have dissipated in a more normal pattern. But, because of the unique shape of the "point" along the Pacific Plate, seismic energy was funneled powerfully toward the center of the Kamchatka Peninsula. Thus, it seems no mere coincidence that the Kamchatka earthquake of 1952 was the most powerful earthquake ever recorded. And, from the standpoint of Bible prophecy — just like the other events that had accompanied the opening of the other seals — the world had been changed forever. Other tests of other bombs eventually produced even more powerful explosions. But, the test of Ivy Mike was the first. Thus, the date of this world-changing event — which also matches *every detail* of the Biblical description — is the date that this writer uses to mark the opening of the sixth seal of Revelation.

Those details continue in Verses 15-17, where John describes the human reaction to the enormous destructive power of the hydrogen bomb. Everyone, from kings to slaves, wanted to hide in caves and holes in the ground, because of the terrible destructive power that had been released when the sixth seal was opened. And, the people realized what was happening, because they concluded that the great day of God's wrath was imminent. In contemplating what had been unleashed, the people asked themselves, "... who is able to stand?"

But, wait, there's more.

"Do not be deceived, God is not mocked; for whatever a man sows, that he will also reap." (Galatians 6:7) Is it possible that the test of Ivy Mike can be tied to the sixth seal in another way? If so, then it would prove definitively that this conclusion is not merely one "of private interpretation". (See: 2nd Peter 1:20) The team that produced thermonuclear weapons showed total dedication to that cause. They sowed unto themselves destruction; that became their life's work.

Destruction is, of course, the opposite of creation. If we go back to the story of the Creation, we notice that "... the Spirit of God was hovering over the face of the waters." (Some translations say, "... moved upon the waters.") The main ingredient in water is hydrogen. The bomb's main explosive ingredient was hydrogen. Nuclear physicist Robert Oppenheimer and his team used the same element that God had used during creation, but reaped destruction from it. They mocked God. And, after witnessing the first explosive test of the atomic bomb — interestingly, code-named Trinity — Oppenheimer famously quoted from the Bhagavad Gita[60]: "If the radiance of a thousand suns were to burst at once into the sky, that would be like the splendor of the mighty one. Now I am become Death[61], the destroyer of worlds."[62] So, as the time approaches for God to redeem Creation, sinful mankind harnesses the most basic element in Creation to reap destruction. The

---

[60] Oppenheimer was — at least, ethnically — a Jew. But, he quoted from the Hindu scriptures. The Hindu goddess of death and destruction is Kali, who was accurately shown in the movie "Indiana Jones and the Temple of Doom". Kali was the huge idol holding the brass cage. Her victims were slowly lowered into a flaming pit. The people that captured her victims were a vicious group called the Thugee, from which we get the word "thug".

[61] A video of Oppenheimer's televised interview — during which, he sheds a tear after uttering the name of the Hindu god Vishnu — can be seen online at: http://www.atomicarchive.com/Movies/Movie8.shtml .

timing of this, and the use of hydrogen, cannot be an accident. Thus, we see how the end of the world is tied to the beginning. This shows the reader the validity of the hydrogen bomb — and not the original atomic bomb — as the event linked to the sixth seal of Revelation.

the big pause

In the Book of Revelation, there is a big pause in events after the opening of the sixth seal. Likewise, this book pauses from the sequential presentation to examine some related events. These events prove beyond any shadow of doubt that there is a God, and that He is in control of Heaven and Earth, and that His Word is true down to the finest level of detail. In fact, the more this writer examined the details of history, and how they fit with the details of the Holy Bible, the more in awe of God this writer became. (Even though this project was started from total awe of God in the first place!)

moving Heaven and Earth

As mentioned in Chapter 1, there were two "tetrads" of solar and lunar eclipses during the 20th Century. Both of those tetrads occurred during years that were significant to the State of Israel: the first when it was founded, and the second when the ancient capital of Jerusalem was liberated from Muslim control.

---

[62] In an interesting side note to Oppenheimer's "marriage" with death, it turns out that one of his atom-bomb co-workers was the lover of Betty Friedan — author, Communist, and pro-abortion activist. Ah, how the cookie crumbles.

At this point, it becomes necessary to address the "who is a Jew?" question. Until recently, this writer hosted a talk-radio program that was heard on a network of 51 stations nationwide. This writer voluntarily terminated the contract with the network, and walked away from the program, because of the bulk of callers (and, likely, network management) that was apparently affiliated with the so-called "Christian Identity" movement. This author asserts that the movement is neither Christian, nor does it have a solid grip on its own identity. They claim to be the "true Israel", but ignore specific Scripture verses that negate their skewed theology. That theology is based upon a hatred of Jews. In order to mask that hatred, they focus intensely on a claim that the people now known colloquially as "Jews" are not the true descendants of the Israelite nation. *Some* of their claims *might* even be true — especially as they apply to the "ethnic, non-practicing Jews"[63] that seem to control the movie industry and the plot content thereof[64]. But, when the Christian Identity crowd tries to claim that the modern State of Israel has no connection to the God of the Bible, then they must blind themselves to the significance of those two tetrads of eclipses.

The reason that the two tetrads are so significant is that even one tetrad had not occurred for *five hundred* years before the revival of Israel.

---

[63] Given that the very definition of a Jew is a person that practices the religion that follows the God of the Bible, and descends from the ancient Hebrews, there is literally no such thing as a "non-practicing Jew". One can call himself that, but it is a skewed term.

[64] Movies often distort Bible verses and doctrine, thus portraying Bible-believing people — Christians and Jews alike — as non-thinking fanatics.

Therefore, two within 20 years is a real "spike" on the celestial event charts! And, given that both tetrads in the 20th Century were tied to significant events in Israel, even the haters of Israel cannot negate the Biblical significance of these events.

Not only did a tetrad not occur for five hundred years, but also the last tetrad was <u>in the year 1492</u>. Although it is well known by little schoolchildren that "Columbus sailed the ocean blue" in that year, there is *far* more to the story. (Herein lies a good reason to home-school your children; or, at least, to have detailed discussions about their public-school lessons over dinner each night[65].)

The next chapter will discuss why the story of Christopher Columbus is so significant to a proper understanding of End Times prophecy. For now, the reader is asked to "skip the details" and consider the larger context of time and Bible timing. Once we have covered that topic more completely, then the story of Christopher Columbus, and the story of the "whore of Babylon"[66], will make much more sense. So will the reader's understanding of Bible prophecy in general, and of End Times prophecy in particular.

---

[65] After reading the next chapter (which began as a mere footnote), you will understand *why* the public-education "establishment" is so afraid of home schooling. You will also understand *why* public-school textbooks maintain <u>the myth</u> that Columbus was searching for a new trade route to India. You will also understand *why* the political Left was so against celebrations of the 500th anniversary of the landing of Columbus in the New World — lest that anniversary should inspire people to <u>study the details of history and thus learn the *truth*</u>. You will also understand why, in early 1992, writer and radio commentator Cal Thomas advised, "Get your children out of the public schools as though they were on fire."

So, also, will the reader's appreciation of the rich details of the Bible (especially in prophecy) increase.

the four winds

Everything in the Bible has meaning. "So shall My word be that goes forth from My mouth; It shall not return to Me void, But it shall accomplish what I please, And it shall prosper in the thing for which I sent it." (Isaiah 55:11) This book began with a mention of the meaning of "leaf" in the Bible. Leaves are blown by the wind. Now, we must examine the meaning, and the action, of wind.[67]

All of Chapter 7 of Revelation concerns itself with the things that John saw after the sixth seal had been opened, but before the seventh seal is opened. If the sixth seal was opened in 1952, then we know that the events of Chapter 7 occur at some point after that. The chapter has a series of events, all of which take place in the spiritual world. The only things that the chapter describes in the physical world are the things that specifically *did not* happen during that time. The winds did not blow upon the earth, the sea, or any tree. The four angels holding back the four winds were instructed not to harm the earth, sea, or trees until another angel had gone throughout the world to mark "the seal of the living God" upon the heads of 144,000 "elect" believers from every tribe of Israel. So, to borrow a favorite quote from Dr. James Dobson

---

[66] Much more on this later in this book. See: Revelation 17-19.

[67] In both Hebrew and Greek, the word "wind" is the same word as "spirit". The Hebrew word is *ru'ach*. The Greek work is *pne'uma*.

(who said this to describe media suppression of important news items), "When nothing is happening, *something* is happening."

Throughout the Bible, "wind" represents God's broad activity in the physical world. There were four main winds that directly affected the people of Israel during the Old Testament period. Those were: 1) the east wind that brought the plague of locusts upon Egypt, 2) the west wind that took the locusts out of Egypt, 3) the east wind that caused the waters of the Red Sea to part and remain walled up during the Exodus; and, 4) the wind that brought the Israelites birds to eat in the wilderness (Numbers 11:31).

After the sixth seal is opened in Revelation, but before the seventh seal is opened, John saw four angels holding back the four winds on Earth. Prior to 1952, as we have just reviewed, there were sweeping changes that affected the entire world. But, after 1952, there has not been another World War. Jet travel had already been invented by 1952 (although it did not become commercially popular until later). Space travel had been planned, and Chuck Yeager had broken the sound barrier (and gone to the edge of space) by then. But, space travel did not affect the whole world, *per se*. Computers and telecommunication had already been invented. The Internet, invented in 1969 by scientists working for the American military (and *not* including Al Gore!), was simply a new combination of technologies that already existed. Islamic terrorism already existed by then. (For example, Hitler had made a pact with the Muslim Brotherhood to enlist their help in eradicating Jews from the face of the earth.) So, from the sixth seal to the seventh, no "wind" of change swept the entire world.

Have there been four winds that affected the people of Israel in the Latter Days? Yes. They were also figurative winds. The first was the "wind" that brought in the stench of Nazi anti-Semitism (just as the first wind brought in the locusts). The second wind was the Allied armies that forced out the Nazis (just as the wind drove out the locusts). The third wind parted the Middle East to revive Israel.

In the Exodus story, the physical third wind blew all night to part the Red Sea and to dry up the sea bottom, so that the Israelites could cross through. Then, the wind kept blowing to hold up the sides of the waters. And, it kept blowing while the Egyptians followed the Israelites into the sea. Then, the wind stopped blowing, and the Egyptians were defeated and drowned.

The modern "wind" blew for a long time, too: from 1948 until 1973. During that time, the Middle East was parted to make room for Israel. Then, as they began to "cross over" — from Germany, from the United States, and from many other parts of the world — the wind kept blowing to support the borders of the new country. Then, after they crossed over, their enemies rushed in to destroy Israel. And, after they were inside Israeli territory, God "closed the waters" upon the enemies of Israel. The "waters" began to close in 1967, when Israel captured Jerusalem. The "waters" finished closing in 1973, when Israel survived a multi-nation, multi-front, war — intended to utterly destroy them — and humiliated the surrounding Arab nations. The 1967 war lasted only six days — the same number of days in which God created the heavens and the earth. The Arab nations launched their 1973 war on Yom Kippur — the Hebrew "day of atonement", when observant

Jews would spend the day in worship and Bible reading. "Awakened" from their contemplation of God, Israel pushed back all of the surrounding enemy nations. The world saw those wars as direct "wind" from God.

And, like the event that happened when the third wind stopped blowing, and the waters of the Red Sea were closed, this modern third wind stopped blowing after the Yom Kippur War. When that war ended, the Egyptians had been humiliated (again), and Israel took possession of the Sinai Peninsula. When the Old Testament third wind stopped blowing, Egypt lost its pharaoh. When the Latter Days third wind stopped blowing, Egypt's president (Anwar Sadat) was assassinated (*ostensibly* by his own people).

In the Old Testament, after they crossed the Red Sea, the Israelites met with God at the mountain[68]. They angered Him by building a golden calf. Did the modern people of Israel anger God in some way after He blew the third wind? Yes!

Instead of taking full control of the land that God had obviously given them, the State of Israel promptly made a deal that gave the Muslims control of the Temple Mount. Just as the ancient Israelites had angered God at a mountain, so did the modern State of Israel.

Moses destroyed the golden calf, and God decided to force Israel to wander in the wilderness as punishment. Even then, God mercifully

---

[68] Although traditionally thought to be Mount Sinai, modern archaeological research indicates that the Mountain of God was really the Harb al-Lawz, a mountain in Saudi Arabia. This is detailed in the book *The Gold of Exodus*.

provided them with manna. But, the people complained to Moses that they wanted to eat meat. God heard their complaints, and blew a wind that brought them birds to eat. But, "while the meat was still between their teeth", God sent a great plague upon the Israelites. The plague was so great that the Israelites named that place "Graves of Craving".

God blew a fourth wind for Israel in the 20th Century, also. It was the series of negotiations (just as there were a series of complaints to Moses) that led up to the 1993 Oslo Peace Accords. When overt, national military force had failed in the two wars (and the outcome cemented world opinion that God was still in the business of blessing Israel), her enemies stepped up acts of localized terrorism. But, instead of utterly destroying her enemies within, the Israelis tried to "tolerate" those enemies. Just as Chapters 19-20 of Leviticus repeat the phrase "do not tolerate" with regard to people that commit certain sexual sins and abominations, the government of Israel should not have tolerated the terrorist-supporting Palestinians within her borders.

A key linguistic note is important here. The word "Palestinian" is a wrong transliteration of the Arabic word. The Arab people of that region, to this day, are called *Philistines* in the Arabic language! The word is written as "*Filistin*" when translating Arabic. This very important point of Biblical understanding has been suppressed by the "lamestream" news media[69], thus keeping the general public from realizing that these are the *same* age-old enemies of Israel that were

---

[69] A wonderfully derisive twist of their self-description as being "mainstream". The term was coined by Joseph Farah, editor and publisher of WorldNetDaily — an American, of Lebanese descent, who speaks Arabic.

written about in the Holy Bible! In fact, the capital of their own "government" is still in Gaza, the ancient capital of the Philistines.

And, that government (the "Palestinian Authority") is the direct political descendant of the Palestine Liberation Organization — the terrorist organization founded by Yasser Arafat.

Just as the people died while eating the birds that they had asked for, the modern State of Israel is dying from the government that had previously enjoyed the benefits of God's "wind" across the battlefield. These modern "birds" (which are sometimes used as symbols of governments in the Bible, such as the "great eagle" that protects the Elect during the Tribulation) are actually warring against their own people — using the Israeli Army to evict the Israeli citizens from the territories negotiated away by the Israeli government to the Filistins! Thus, their meat (the army) has become poisonous to modern Israel.

Just as God was angry with the Israelites for wanting to go back and negotiate with their Egyptian oppressors, God is now allowing the Israeli government to negotiate away its own existence. Even part of the hard-won control of Jerusalem is being given away to the Filistins, to whom the Israelis gave control of the Temple Mount shortly after liberating Jerusalem in 1967. Imagine how angry God must be!

the seventh seal

The actual signing of the 1993 Oslo "Peace" Accords (and that famous photograph) is the event linked with the opening of the seventh seal of Revelation. The "great plague" that fell upon modern Israel "while the meat was still between their teeth" was the series of Filistin uprisings that led to Israel evicting their own people from Judea and Samaria[70]. Further, the opening of the seventh seal causes two events in the spiritual world. First, it ushers in a period of "silence in Heaven". That silence lasts for "about half an hour". (Revelation 8:1) Silence seems to be an unusual event in Heaven (where saints and angels continually praise God). So, we must define the duration of "half an hour" in Heaven.

After the silence in Heaven, there is a period of loud noise. Special angels blow special trumpets. We know that these angels are special because John designates them as "the seven angels that stand before God". (Rev. 8:2) Another angel burns extra incense before the altar of God at this point, and the seven special angels "prepared themselves" to sound their trumpets. Thus, we know that the seventh seal causes a time of preparation in Heaven for the dramatic events that will occur on Earth when the seven trumpets are blown.

At the point when the seventh seal was opened, time passed from the Latter Days into the End Times. There was not much time from the seventh seal to the beginning of The Tribulation.[71] How much time?

silence in Heaven

Our clue about the length of "half an hour" comes from 2nd Peter 3:8, which is quoted at the beginning of this chapter. We discover that

---

[70] Euphemistically called "The West Bank" by the same lamestream media.
[71] This sentence was changed to past tense for the 4th Edition.

time does, indeed, compress between Heaven and Earth. We learn that, "... with the Lord one day is as a thousand years, and a thousand years as one day." So, just how long is that? If we take 1,000, and divide it by 48 (the number of half-hours in one day), we get 20.83 years. This number does *not* change between the Hebrew and Gregorian calendars, because the unit of measure is years, and not months.[72]

However, it is important to note that the text says "about" half an hour.

The Greek word used, *hos*, has several related meanings. The meaning that Bible translators have used is "something like". So, the silence in Heaven lasts "something like" half an hour. That would mean more or less a 21-year period.

At this point, we will revert to "back-timing" to see if there is a significant point in the history of Israel that matches the Scriptural time references. We know that Jesus gave a list of specific signs in the sky, and that those signs (the "tetrad" of eclipses) would occur *after* The Tribulation. We know that the tetrad begins in the Spring of 2014, and lasts for one year. We do not know *which* set of eclipses, or the entire tetrad, Jesus mentioned as His time reference point. But, we do know that the tetrad marks the *end* of The Tribulation. Given that

---

[72] As noted earlier, the Hebrew calendar has 360 days, while the Gregorian calendar has 365 days. Each calendar has its own system for reconciling the difference between recorded days and the precise solar year. The Hebrew calendar occasionally adds a "leap month", while the Gregorian calendar adds a "leap day". Solar years, however, have certain measurable points of fixed reference. These fixed references will become more important as this examination continues to unfold later in this book.

the tetrad is such an unusual event, and given the timing of the last tetrad, we will assume that the entire year-long event is significant.

If the tetrad ends in 2015, then The Tribulation *starts* in 2008.

And, if the Great Tribulation (the second half of the seven-year Tribulation) is marked by the reign of The Antichrist over all the Earth, then something happens in late 2011 or early 2012 that will usher in that global reign of terror. But, is there any proof for this grand assumption about the reign of The Antichrist and its relation to the tetrad of solar and lunar eclipses?

Almost twenty years (or, "about half an hour") prior to the predicted time of the reign of The Antichrist, the modern State of Israel began the process of giving away its own hard-won territory to her enemies. That process came via the Oslo Peace Accords, which were signed on 13 September 1993 in Oslo, Norway. The famous photo of President Bill Clinton "brokering" the peace accords memorialized a turning point in world history. Some cried, "Peace! Peace!" But, there is no peace. Instead, the Oslo Peace Accords ushered in the "intifada" that led to the formation of a Filistin government within modern Israel.

Just as described earlier in this book, the "wind" had stopped blowing in favor of Israel after the 1973 Six-Day War. After the 1993 "peace" accords, it seems that there was "silence in Heaven". In other words, no true prophetic utterance about the nation of Israel has been given since Israel literally shook hands with a Filistin — Yasser Arafat — <u>and thus turned her back on God's protection and provision.</u>

Israel makes "peace" with her ancient enemy, the Philistines
(What role will Bill Clinton[73] play in Tribulation political events?)
Photo source: Wikipedia Commons (public domain)

Has the seventh seal of Revelation already been opened? Has the silence in Heaven almost ended? Has the angel thrown down the fire from Heaven? Have the accompanying events already occurred? And, is there something else that accompanied the opening of the seal?

We shall address that final question first. The angel told Daniel that knowledge of prophetic events would be sealed up "until the time of the end". As the seals of the scroll were opened, more and more detailed understanding of End Times prophecy has poured out upon mankind. In this writer's opinion, it is no mere coincidence that the modern interest in End Times knowledge began in 1973 — as Hal Lindsey's key book, *The Late, Great Planet Earth* swept around the

---

[73] Go online, and view a high-resolution version of this photograph. Note the similarity of the pattern of Clinton's necktie to that of Arafat's headscarf. It is well known that Clinton used visual imagery to convey political signals. The Oslo "Peace" Accords ushered in the erosion of Israel's security. Yet, many misguided Jews thought that Clinton was "on their side". More on that later.

world — just as the "wind" swept across Israel after the sixth seal was opened.

Imagine a physical scroll with seven seals. As each seal is broken open, portions of the written word inside begin to appear. In other words, a little bit of the knowledge inside "leaks out" as each seal is opened. With the first few seals, that leak is very small. But, when only the last two seals remain, enough of the page would be visible that a discerning reader might begin to realize what is written inside. Thus it is that, even as the Latter Days were already upon us, few realized the Biblical timing of world events ... until recently.

Revelation 8:5 says that the angel threw fire from Heaven to the Earth. That produced "noises, thunderings, lightnings, and an earthquake". Notice that the sounds produced were on Earth. Apparently, the angel throwing fire to the Earth is a precursor event. There is still silence in Heaven as the seven special angels *prepare* to blow their trumpets.

As this book is being written, events are already unfolding. The specific research for this book began in early 2008. But, this writer has been reading and examining Bible prophecy for decades. As certain information becomes known (such as the alternative meaning for the "beasts of the earth"), and certain events happen (such as some voters proclaiming that Barack Obama really is The Messiah), some long-held views of this writer have been forced to change. This writer is dedicated to a pursuit of Bible truth, not to a pursuit of doctrine or denomination. This book is dedicated to revealing the results of the research, in hopes that many souls will be saved while there is still time. And, the evidence discovered shows that time *is* running out.

In fact, according to this writer's calculations, the precursor event for the earthquake — the last End Times event before the first angel blows his trumpet, and thus begins The Tribulation — *already occurred* on Friday, the 20th of June 2008. The precursor was the fire being thrown from the altar of God down to Earth. That triggered the California wildfires. As this is being typed, this writer believes that the heat from the wildfires will affect the subterranean rock formations and thus cause an earthquake. Just as earthquakes normally have a precursor event, this earthquake will be the final precursor event before the "official" start of The Tribulation via the first trumpet.

But, on 12 May 2008, an unusual earthquake happened. That earthquake, in central China, happened in a place that was not near any known fault zones. In other words, it happened in an "earthquake safe" area. And, it happened only two days before the 60th anniversary of the founding of the modern State of Israel. Some people thought that earthquake was significant. But, it did *not* follow the Scriptural sequence. In order to prove that it is the event in Revelation, an earthquake would need to be associated with fires, which themselves were associated with "fire from Heaven".

Jesus said that "this generation" that sees the fig tree put forth its leaves, "... will not pass away until all these things take place." Israel was founded in May of 1948. A generation is 60 years, not 40 years as many have supposed in the past. (The "generation" of Israelites that wandered in the wilderness was the generation that "had sinned" by building the golden calf. The Bible specifies that only those over the age of 20 years would die in the wilderness. So, those who were alive during The Passover, but were less than 20 years old when the golden calf was built, were "the generation" that entered the Promised Land. They would have been up to 60 years old, having wandered for the entire 40 years. Thus, the "generation" that was alive when modern Israel was revived is 60 years old *right now!*[74])

All of the seals have been opened. The first trumpet sounded last year, and the others are about to sound.[75]

John wrote in Revelation 22:18-19 that no one should add or take away even "one word" of his prophecy. We have just seen the effect of the word "about". It shows how the period from September of 1993 until June of 2008 equals "about" half an hour in Heaven. We will now examine the word "prepared" in Revelation 8:6, when the seven angels "prepared themselves" to blow the seven trumpets that start the first half of The Tribulation.

The Greek word used is *hetoimazo*, meaning "to prepare" or "to make the necessary arrangements". It comes from the noun *heteos*, meaning "fitness". The Lexicon explains that *hetoimazo* draws on a metaphor of sending people ahead of a king to make the road level or passable.

---

[74] For a more detailed explanation of the length of a generation, click onto: http://www.watchmanbiblestudy.com/BibleStudies/HIStoryOurFuture_14000Days.htm

[75] The grammatical tense has been altered from the 1st Edition, to show the progression of time. The first trumpet blast is no longer in the future.

Thus, when the angels "prepared themselves" it was not a momentary effort; it required a period of time. But, how much time?

The Bible is technically silent on the topic; but, there are clues that this writer believes give us a reliable framework for the time of preparation. The period is 96 days. Here is the explanation.

From the date of the wildfires (Fri, 20 Jun 2008) until the date of this year's Feast of Trumpets (Mon, 29 Sep 2008) is 92 days. The fires were ignited by lightning ("fire from Heaven") exactly three days (the time that Jesus spent in "the heart of the earth") after the California Supreme Court overturned the ballot resolution that banned homosexual "marriage" in that state. So, from that fateful court decision until the Feast of Trumpets is 95 days. Add one for the difference between the calculation of the Hebrew calendar (on which days begin at sunset the day before they do on the Christian calendar), and one arrives at 96 days. In Hebrew numerology, eight is the number of The Messiah. There are twelve tribes of Israel. Twelve times eight equals 96 days. The angels in Heaven are preparing to blow the other trumpets[76], to prepare Israel (the people of God) for the soon return of Yeshua Ha'Meshiach (Jesus the Christ). The trumpets will blow *simultaneously* in Heaven and on Earth! (And, that date is exactly seven years from the start of the next Year of Jubilee.)

The Feast of Trumpets is called *Rosh Hashanna* in Hebrew. (NOTE: In the 1st and 2nd Editions of this book, I erroneously said that the Feast

---

[76] The text has been slightly altered from the 1st Edition, to show the progression of time. The first trumpet blast is no longer in the future.

of Trumpets coincides with the Festival of Booths, *Succoth*. My error was reported to me by a Messianic reader. Hence, the 3rd Edition.)

The Feast of Trumpets is two days long. Add those two days to the 96 days from the court decision until the start of the festival, and one gets 98 days. Divide 98 days in half, and one gets 49 days. It was exactly 49 days (seven weeks) from the day of the infamous California court decision (their Supreme Court is located in Sacramento, the state capital) until an earthquake struck Sacramento. Thus, the earthquake fulfilled the final portion of John's prophecy in Revelation 8:5. But, is there more? I believe so.

Three days after the lightning storm ignited the wildfires, I began a new online column series called The Crossbow. (Named for the long-range weapon that could pierce personal body armor on the ancient battlefield. The Holy Cross can reach across the long ranges of time, distance, and spiritual void, and can pierce the hardness that Satan's lies can build up around the human heart.) Several of the columns in the series show how the court decision, the lightning storm, the wildfires, and the earthquake are related. (This author — simply by observing the signs in the Holy Bible — predicted the earthquake *weeks* in advance. Seismologists can only predict quakes hours in advance, if at all.) The column series also showed — using real-time earthquake maps from the US Geological Survey — a distinctive "reverse crescent" pattern of earthquake foreshocks. The Crescent and Star together form the symbol for Islam. But, this pattern of quakes put the Crescent and Star in an upside-down and backwards position. In religious iconography, that forms an extreme insult. Not only that, but the same "reverse crescent" pattern was seen in the locations of the wildfires that preceded the earthquakes — and in the *same* areas of Northern California!

While the reverse Crescent marked the locations of both the fires and the earthquakes, the location of the star was also significant. When the Crescent and Star are turned upside-down and backwards, the star is located on the map *precisely* over a place called the Bohemian Grove.

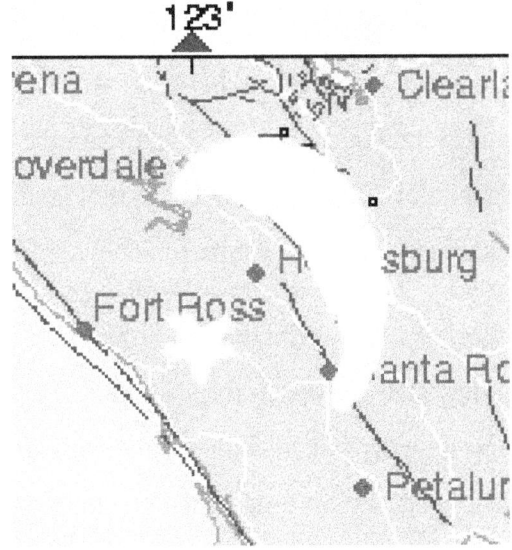

Islamic "Crescent and Star" — upside-down and backwards!
Both the fires and earthquakes were heaviest in crescent area.
Satanic upside-down star marks location of idol at Bohemian Grove.
(from USGS real-time earthquake map, with quakes shaded in)

This author had heard of the Bohemian Grove since the mid-1990s, but did not believe the tales about world leaders and idol worship there. Then, videojournalist Alex Jones penetrated the security of the Grove, and recorded the pagan "Cremation of Care" ceremony. It occurs before a 30-foot idol of an owl, which is the symbol of the Bohemian Club that owns the Grove. Older translations of the Holy Bible (such as the King James Version) translate the name of the Sumerian demon Lillith as an owl (specifically, a "screech owl"). The Sumerians were among a number of peoples and empires that inhabited the vast Mesopotamian Plain where modern Iraq (and part of Iran) is now located. And, the demon Lillith persists in the mythology of many peoples beyond Mesopotamia. Places where Lillith appears in local myths include the British Isles. Great Britain (especially Scotland) is the birthplace of the Freemasons, from which come many government leaders. Thus, there is a spiritual link between at least one demon of Mesopotamia and the Freemasons.[77] Leaders from the worlds of business, government, and the news media come together for pagan rituals at the Bohemian Grove each summer.

As we will see, there is a direct link between the court decision, the lightning storm, the wildfires, the earthquake, and ... certain dates on the calendar, along with the pagan rituals at the Bohemian Grove. Because of the leap year, the Summer Solstice came one day earlier this year than it normally does. That date was the 20th of June — the exact date of the California lightning storm. That date was a Friday, on which the Jewish Sabbath starts at sunset. Thus, the first Sabbath after the California court decision was marred by the wildfires.

The ancient Julian calendar (invented by Julius Caesar) is 13 days out of synch with the modern Gregorian calendar (invented by Pope

---

[77] There are others, as we will see later.

Gregory the 13th). The Julian calendar was in use at the time of Jesus. Thus, on the day when the 20th of June would be marked on the Julian calendar, it is the 3rd of July on the modern Gregorian calendar. The 3rd of July, in turn, marks the appearance of the "dog star", Sirius. That, in turn, marks the start of the "Dog Days of Summer" — the hottest period of each year.

It is during the Dog Days each year that the pagan rituals occur at the Bohemian Grove. The wildfires form a virtual half-ring around the Bohemian Grove. Lillith was worshipped by the cultures in Mesopotamia, the land from which God called out Abraham. The word "holy" means "set apart from" or "called out of". God is seeking a holy people. Can this country be holy, when its leaders[78] — from business, government, and the major news media — make plans among themselves while worshipping an idol of an owl?! The Bohemian Grove participants keep a lid on events that might blow the cover off the pagan nature of certain government policies, etc. So, it would only make sense that God would begin The Tribulation in a way that marks the punishments as being connected to the crimes. The only problem is that the connections have been hidden from the public. No wonder. The key people from the news agencies that should be watchdogs of our leaders are co-participants in those pagan rituals.

---

[78] Membership has included David Rockefeller, Henry Kissinger, Walter Cronkite, Richard Nixon, "captains of industry", and the owners of several major newspapers. Membership is only by recommendation, after a detailed application. Notably, the waiting list is 33 years long — the same number of years that Jesus lived on Earth. Coincidence? (In addition to the Alex Jones video, see: "Masters of the Universe go to Camp: Inside the Bohemian Grove", by Phillip Weiss, *Spy* magazine, Nov 1989, pp. 59-76.)

Do calendars and dates really matter in Christian prophecy? Yes!

There is a concept among Christian scholars called the Six-Day Week. It is based upon the verse quoted at the beginning of this chapter, that "with the Lord, one day is as a thousand years, and a thousand years is as one day". Here is the "short version" of the concept. God created the world and everything in it in six days. Then, He rested on the seventh day. On that seventh day, Eve sinned first[79] by acting upon the advice of the serpent. Then, Adam sinned by acting upon the advice of Eve. (Then, God cursed Adam, "... *because* you have heeded the voice of your wife".[80] Genesis 3:17.) In order to undo the damage done by sin, God made a way out. But, the people chosen to lead the way out themselves went astray. So, God made a better way out by sending His Son to lead the way out of sin. That entire process of undoing the damage done to Creation[81] would "redeem the time"[82] by taking the same amount of time. But, as this entire chapter explains, time in Heaven is not necessarily the same as time on Earth. God measured out six days to work His plan of salvation. Then, after the final triumph of good over evil[83], those who *fully* believe in the

---

[79] Genesis 3:6.

[80] Not many preachers point out *that* fact, either, for fear that women will stop putting money in the collection plates! Yet, our government "leaders" want to put women in leadership roles in government and even combat. That condition of female "leadership" is a self-imposed *curse*. See: Isaiah 3:12, and compare that with 1st Corinthians 14:34.

[81] See: Romans 5:12.

[82] See: Ephesians 5:16.

[83] Armageddon: the battle in the Valley of Megiddo, when Satan is defeated.

God of the Bible[84] will accompany Jesus into Heaven to enter into His rest[85]. That final rest will be eternal. It will be the seventh day of the week of the age of man. It will be unlike the other six days, which are each one thousand years, just as the seventh day of Creation was unlike the other six days. God knew the end from the beginning.

Christian scholars note that — according to the Six-Day Week scenario — Jesus appeared on Earth in the flesh at the point of Holy Week[86] at which animals of flesh appeared in Creation Week, the fifth day[87]. Jesus saved mankind by his death on the day that mankind was given life, the sixth day. (Consider, for example, that the Last Supper began just after sundown on Thursday of Holy Week — thus fitting precisely the Six-Day Week scenario, even with regard to the very first Holy Communion as an act of the "re-creation" — via His redemptive sacrifice — of mankind on the sixth day.) Jesus descended into Hell on the day mankind descended into sin, the seventh day. Jesus rose from the dead on the *eighth* day that He was in Jerusalem. In the Hebrew system of Biblical numerology, eight is the number of The Messiah. (Remember that eight [The Messiah] times 12 [tribes] equals 96 days from the court decision to the end of the Festival of Booths.)

---

[84] and *not* in some non-descript "great moosh god", with no Son, to borrow a phrase from Nashville talk-radio host Michael DelGiorno.

[85] See: Matthew 11:29, and Hebrews 3:18 and 4:11

[86] The final week that Jesus spent in Jerusalem, from the triumph over man's government on Palm Sunday to triumph over death on Resurrection Day.

[87] See: Galatians 4:4, about "the fullness of time".

According to the best analyses of recorded history, civilization is six thousand years old. We are at the end of the Six-Day Week. But, this time, Jesus will not descend into Hell. (While there after the Crucifixion, He set the captives free!) Instead, Jesus will descend from Heaven to Earth, and then send Satan and his angels into Hell.

Then, just as God rested on the seventh day after the six days of Creation, and Jesus spent the seventh day of Holy Week in the tomb, there will be one day (one thousand years) of rest here on Earth. That period is commonly called The Millennium. That is when the followers of Jesus will "rule and reign" with Jesus here on Earth. Then will follow the *eternal* eighth day — the Kingdom of God, contained in the New Heaven and the New Earth described in the final part of Revelation. Holy Week is sometimes called the Eight-Day Week, because Jesus actually spent eight days in Jerusalem (from Palm Sunday until Resurrection Day, inclusive). Thus, Jesus will have "redeemed the time" after Satan suffers final defeat at Armageddon.

The total period, in "Bible time", from the creation of the world until the Battle of Armageddon is exactly six days! The seventh day will be The Millennium, which follows The Great Tribulation.

But, wait, there's more!

For those that cannot believe in Bible interpretation unless it has some direct connection to worldly events and lives, there are interesting "factoids" that could help the reader make such connections. First, the Gregorian calendar is 13 days out of synch from the Julian calendar, which was in use by the Roman government that occupied Jerusalem at the time the Jesus stood before their local governor, Pontius Pilate. Second, there are 13 days from the Summer Solstice until the start of the Dog Days of Summer.

During the administration of President Bill Clinton, many people (this writer included) thought that he could be the man that becomes The Antichrist. When that didn't happen <u>*during* his administration</u>, many people thought that was the end of it. Now, presidential candidate Senator Barack Obama[88] is under the proverbial microscope, largely because of his support for homosexuals and for an Islamic dialogue.

Keep in mind that The Antichrist is put into place by a precursor (there's that word again...). He is known as The False Prophet. Just as John the Baptizer[89] was a precursor for Jesus, The False Prophet will be a precursor for The Antichrist. The Antichrist and the False Prophet will both serve the Father of Lies.

Barack Obama was raised as a Muslim, but he now claims to be a Christian. But, he has never publicly renounced Islam. So — according to the definitions of Christianity, Islam, and Judaism — Barack Obama is still a Muslim. But, he is also known to carry a Hindu idol in his pocket "for luck". Given his ability to woo the crowds with his speaking skills, Obama would be a good candidate for

---

[88] **4th Edition** footnote: he was inaugurated as president — despite being disqualified by his Kenyan birth — on 20 January 2009, a crescent moon.

[89] A more correct term, which avoids confusion with the Baptist denomination of Christianity. John went forth baptizing — thus, he was a "Baptizer", but he was not a "Baptist" in the modern sense of the term.

The False Prophet. If he were elected president, then he would be in a position to appoint Bill Clinton as the US ambassador to the United Nations. Once there, Clinton would be likely to become elected as secretary-general. That would, according to the worldly standard, effectively make him "king of the world". As such, he could easily become The Antichrist.

Bill Clinton and Barack Obama have several things in common. In addition to their support for homosexuality and abortion, and their disdain for traditional Christian values, they also have a hidden link. Bill Clinton was born on 19 August 1946. Barack Obama was born on 04 August 1961. On the Gregorian calendar, they were born 15 days apart (*and* 15 *years* apart). But, on the *Hebrew* Calendar, both men share the *same* birthdate: the 22nd of Av. Hebrew tradition tells us that the 9th of Av is a bad day in history. Among other things, both Temples were destroyed on the 9th of Av. The common birthdate of Clinton and Obama is <u>13 days</u> after the 9th of Av! Coincidence?

With all of that information in mind, let's look again at the events of Friday, 20 June 2008. It was the Summer Solstice. But, it was not a normal Solstice. Because 2008 was a leap year[90], the Solstice was one day earlier than usual. And, it fell on a Friday, the start of the Jewish Sabbath. And, the nation of Israel conducted a massive military exercise that day — to prepare for a possible pre-emptive strike against Iran's nuclear facilities. The wildfires in California started that day. French president Nicolas Sarkozy, while visiting Israel, was

---

[90] In the 4th Edition (Feb 2009), this paragraph was updated for tense.

under fear of assassination when a policeman reportedly killed himself nearby. And, it was 13 days until the start of the Dog Days.

And ... a company called Nordic ID introduced a handheld scanner that it boasts can read an RFID chip from 13 feet away. (Can you say "mark of the Beast" and "security checkpoint" in the same sentence? Now you can.) If the reader is not aware of how RFID chips can be implanted in the human body, it is highly advisable to learn quickly.

Three days after that significant date, former president Bill Clinton gave a speech endorsing Barack Obama for president. Previously, Bill Clinton had been critical of Obama, and had supported his wife, Senator Hillary Clinton, for president. Notably, Hillary Clinton had not formally withdrawn her candidacy; she had only *suspended* her campaign, after Obama won enough delegates to become the "presumptive" Democratic Party nominee.[91]

recap

The time of the first six seals was the time period of the Latter Days. The time period of the seventh seal, including the "silence in Heaven", was the time period of the End Times. We are now moving into the first half of that seven-year period known as The Tribulation. The specific event that marks the transition toward the actual beginning of

---

[91] Note for 3rd Edition: when this book was first released in August of 2008, scoffers rejected this entire concept by claiming that conservative voters would "save America". Now that the election is over, and Barack Obama has won that election, talk-radio is abuzz with talk of Bible prophecy and the role that Obama could have therein. In one day (the 3rd Edition was released on Wed, 05 Nov, the day after the election), book sales have risen accordingly.

The Tribulation is the angel taking fire from the altar of God and throwing it down to Earth.[92] That event in Heaven triggered a precise sequence of events on Earth. Specifically, a lightning storm that triggered wildfires that triggered earthquakes — all in the area between Sacramento (where the court decision to resume same-sex "marriage" was made) and the site of the idol at the Bohemian Grove.

It is exactly 96 days (8 x 12) from that fateful court decision until the end of the Feast of Trumpets. The 8x12 refers to the Hebrew number for The Messiah, times the number of tribes of Israel. The very next event described in Revelation, after the earthquake caused by the fire from Heaven, is the blowing of the first of seven trumpets. <u>The Tribulation began when the first trumpet sounded</u>.[93] This author believes that the first trumpet sounded in Heaven at the exact same time as this year's Festival of Trumpets here on Earth.[94] From that date, it will be exactly seven years (the same period as The Tribulation) until the start of the next Year of Jubilee on the Hebrew Calendar. The Bible says that, when The Messiah begins His reign on Earth, it will be the beginning of a Year of Jubilee.

---

[92] Some translations say "into the Earth", which carries even more resonance with regard to the wildfires heating up the rock formations to trigger the earthquakes in the same vicinity. For a scientific explanation of how outside forces can influence underground rock formations, and thus trigger quakes, see the Syzygy newsletter (by a retired geologist) at: www.syzygyjob.com

[93] In the **4th Edition** (Feb 2009), this paragraph was updated for tense.

[94] The official start of the Feast of Trumpets each year on the Hebrew calendar is the appearance of the New Moon at sunset, as seen from the Temple Mount in Jerusalem, to begin the date of the 1st of Tishri.

This author has studied Bible prophecy since 1973, and has never seen a time when all of the signs lined up so perfectly with every detail of the prophecies in the Holy Bible.

the end of time

The point of this chapter is that time, and the measurement of time, have changed ... as time goes by. In ancient times, years were marked as they relate to the reign of a particular king. The modern calendar moves forward from a fixed point in history.[95] The Israelite calendar is based upon lunar months, and has 360 days. The Christian (Gregorian) calendar is based upon solar years, and has 365 days. Ancient cultures — such as the Egyptians, Mayans, and Druids — built structures that were apparently used to calculate celestial events. Those structures were built with amazing precision. Obviously, time has been an important factor in human civilizations.

But, time has changed. The difference between the 360-day, lunar-based system and the 365-day, solar-based system is not without its own questions. Which one is right? Is it possible that both are right? And, if only one is right, then was there some specific event that changed the entire Earth in some way that caused the recalculation of the measurement of time? And, if so, then what was it? Actually, there were two events. Both, of course, are recorded in the Bible.

The first occurred in the 10th chapter of the Book of Joshua, when God caused the sun and moon to stand still in the sky for "about a whole

---

[95] Of course, that fixed point is the birth of Jesus — the King of the Universe.

day"[96], so that the Israelites could complete God's revenge upon their enemies. The second event occurred in the 38th chapter of the Book of Isaiah, when God caused the sun to move backward as a sign to King Hezekiah that He had heard the king's prayers and would extend his life by 15 years[97]. For the mathematical and astronomical details of how this could happen, and the effect upon the length of days (via the rotational speed of Earth's orbit around the Sun, combined with the Moon's orbit around the Earth), read the "360 vs. 365" papers by Guy Cramer[98]. He shows, with amazing mathematical precision, that it *is* possible to measure the changes that God made in the rotations of the Earth and the Moon in order to cause the events described in the Bible.

But, in order to usher in the perfect world that will be ruled by Yeshua Ha'Meshiach, there will need to be another astronomical correction. That will return the Earth from a solar year of 365.24 days per year to a perfect 360 days per year. That could require a cataclysmic event.

---

[96] There's that word "about" again. And, again, dealing with a time period.

[97] The same length of time as the age difference between Bill Clinton and Barack Obama, and the length of time between the opening of the seventh seal (the signing of the Oslo "Peace" Accords in September of 1993) and the Feast of Trumpets in September of 2008. (On the Hebrew calendar, the accords were signed on the 23rd of Elul 5753, and the latest Feast of Trumpets began on the 1st of Tishri 5769. The difference, on the Hebrew calendar, from the 23rd of Elul until the 1st of Tishri is exactly seven days.

News stories that have recently appeared during the final editing of this book (August, 2008) show that there are new links between Bill Clinton and Barack Hussein Obama. Both men have questions surrounding their birth and childhood. Both had early changes in their fathers. Both have names with prophetic significance. And, both have strong ties to Communism.

[98] at: http://www.direct.ca/trinity/360vs365.html

Notably, just such an event is the very next thing in the Biblical sequence. As noted before, this event will usher in The Tribulation.

Notably, the 13-day period mentioned earlier — between the Summer Solstice and the start of the Dog Days of 2008 — contains the 100th anniversary of the "Tunguska Event". That was the cataclysmic explosion over western Siberia[99]. Some scientists think that it was caused by an asteroid impact. But, no fragments have ever been found. The event flattened mature forests — with the fallen trees radiating outward from a central point — over 800 square miles.

The results of the Tunguska Event bear a remarkable similarity to the events described in Revelation 8:7, after an angel blows the first of the seven trumpets. That event will be unmistakable, because it will affect one-third of the earth and the trees, plus all of the green grass. And, it will have a unique identifying feature ("hail and fire, mixed with blood"), so that no one can say it is anything other than what it is.

Matthew 24:1-22 lists signs leading up to Jesus' return. It follows the sequence of Revelation precisely. Then, in Verse 23, Jesus begins a warning about how to avoid being misled during the Latter Days and the End Times. The key to avoiding the troubles that await unbelievers is to avoid following a "false Christ" or a "false prophet". The ultimate goal of this book is that — by learning to read the Bible

---

[99] **30 June 1908**. The event is described in many different sources. (See the 4th Edition notes in the Afterword for a description of an event of a similar event that happened shortly after the release of the 1st Edition of this book.)

in a detailed and integrated way — the reader will get to know the true Jesus better, both in this world and in the next.

We will compare the true Christ to "many false Christs". But, first, just as there is a pause and a preparation before the trumpets sound, this book will pause to examine an oft-overlooked point of preparation for the understanding of End Times prophecies.

Chapter 3: Up From the Depths

Schoolchildren have long been taught that Christopher Columbus was motivated by money, and that he was seeking a cheaper route for the transport of spices and other goods from the Far East (via water, instead of the Silk Road). The myth says that a young Christopher concluded that the Earth is round because he saw the masts of the ships getting taller as they came closer to the shore from far out in the ocean. For that myth to be true, then: a) no one else in the history of ship travel would've noticed that phenomenon, b) ancient Greek maps — which depict the Earth as round — would need to be ignored, and c) a young boy would need to sit still and pay attention for long periods of time regularly. Can there be another explanation?

The very name Christopher means "bearer of Christ". Could it be that the boy's parents gave him that name for a reason? And, if so, then what was that reason? And, if the young Christopher Columbus was taught from a young age that he was supposed to "bear" Christ, then where was he supposed to go? And, if Christopher Columbus had a true "mission in life" to bear Christ to a foreign land, then was he able to convey that concept to anyone that would help him in that mission?

The answer will "rock your world", and prove that even some of the most basic lessons of history in public schools have been skewed to show a minimal influence of Jesus the Christ upon world events.

According to research in the mid-1980s by Dr. D. James Kennedy[100], the diary of Christopher Columbus reveals some amazing facts that show how little of the modern story about Columbus is true. Young Christopher grew up in a seafaring family. They were also devout Christians, as testified by the name given to the famed explorer.

As the story told by Dr. Kennedy goes, there was a monk in Europe that was well known for having God's gift of healing. This monk would travel from town to town and heal the sick in the name of Jesus. But, during that period, Muslims had invaded Spain from North Africa, having already conquered much of that continent in the name of *their* god, Allah. (Another myth is that Allah is the same god as Yehowah[101].) A group of Muslims had heard about this monk, and had set out to stop him from ministering in the name of Yeshua (Jesus). They captured him, and then they snuck him out of Spain on a ship. They had planned to toss him overboard in the ocean. But,

---

[100] A noted Bible scholar, and founder of Coral Ridge Ministries. See more at: http://www.coralridge.org

[101] The correct transliteration, commonly rendered "Jehovah" in English, of the "proper name" of God. This is the name declared to Moses at the burning bush. The name means "I am that I am", and is often written in capital letters simply as "I AM". During one of this writer's talk-radio broadcasts, a Muslim caller wanted to discuss Islam from the perspective that "we all worship the same God". I asked, "Then why do you call him Allah, instead of Yehowah?" The caller was stunned that I had used that particular name and pronunciation, because he had studied the Quran in a school in West Africa. He had learned Arabic for his Quranic studies, and had also learned some of the native language of that country. When I said "Yehowah", he responded, "Ah, the Self-Existent One!" In that country, Yehowah was known by that name from ancient times; but, the caller had never picked up on the idea that Yehowah and Allah cannot be the same. For more details about this, do a Net search of this writer's name and the phrase "their god is at war with our God".

because he was a man of God, they decided to put him afloat on a board. (Thus, if he truly was a representative of God, then God could save him.)

A ship captain was taking cargo from Spain to somewhere in Africa. The ship's watchman spotted something floating in the ocean. It was a man on a board. The captain diverted the ship from its course to rescue the man. When the man was brought aboard, the captain recognized him as that famous monk. The monk was near dead, and asked the captain to remain with him and listen to the story of a vision that the monk had been given while floating alone in the ocean. God had shown the monk that there was an entire part of the Earth that had never been given an opportunity to hear the good news about Jesus the Christ. The monk described that the Earth was a sphere, and that ships would not fall off the edge of the world as popularly believed. Dr. Kennedy concluded his presentation by revealing that the captain of the ship was Stefan Columbus, the *grand*father of Christopher.

With that in mind, the reader can now see that young Christopher — if he did actually sit on the dock and stare off to the west — *did not* merely conclude *by accident* that the Earth was a sphere. He would've had his grandfather's stories in mind. Thus, he had confidence that there was a New World somewhere on the other side of the ocean. The question in his mind would've been how to reach it — not whether it existed, nor whether it could be reached. Christopher would've been praying to God for guidance regarding the task of reaching the New World beyond the Atlantic Ocean, not just guessing.

But, wait, there's more ... much more. And, yes, these details *do* have an effect on our understanding of near-future Bible prophecy events.

It is not only significant *where* Columbus wanted to go. It is also significant *when* he left. And, it is significant *how* he got there, and exactly *where* "there" was, and *what* he did when he arrived. Read on.

Christopher Columbus was a man with a true 'mission in life"; his name reminded him daily. Therefore, it should be no surprise that he was able to speak passionately and convincingly enough to recruit enough stout-hearted sailors to "boldly go where no man had gone before", and to avoid the mutiny that surely would've accompanied a mission to fall off the edge of the planet.

Because he knew that his primary mission was to "bear Christ" to the New World (and not to bring back spices, which *might* have been a secondary mission), he named his ships accordingly: the Niña, the Pinta, and the Santa Maria (the Baby, the Donkey, and Saint Mary). Just as those three bore Christ to His birth in a new world (the physical world, as opposed to the spiritual world), so these three ships would bear Christ to the New World. It really is so simple, yet sophisticated.

Columbus' crew sighted land and came ashore on 12 October 1492. But, scholars are unclear as to exactly where he came ashore[102]. There was a certain amount of wandering, exploration, and interaction with the island natives. The captain of the Pinta broke away from the other

---

[102] see "The Columbus Landfall Homepage", at:
http://www.columbusnavigation.com/cclandfl.shtml

two ships during that period, supposedly in search of gold. The ship ran aground on Christmas Day. So, the crew built a fort on the island of Hispaniola ("Little Spain"), and they called the fort La Navidad ("Christmas"). Columbus and his remaining men also landed on Hispaniola, restocked their ship, and set off to return to Spain from the eastern end of the island of Hispaniola. This location is significant.

Jesus came into this world, traveled it for a period of time, foretold that He would leave, and promised that He would return. Columbus did likewise. The departure of Jesus from this world is an event called The Ascension. By visibly ascending back into Heaven, after having arisen from the dead, Jesus proved that He was what He had claimed to be. By returning to Spain, Columbus proved that his mission was everything that he had foretold it to be. By the glorious Ascension, Jesus waved His victory banner over Hell and bridged the gap between Earth and Heaven. Is there a parallel for the journey of Columbus?

Just off the eastern end of the island of Hispaniola is the deepest point of the entire Atlantic Ocean: the Milwaukee Deep[103], an area of the Puerto Rico Trench. It is approximately 28,000 feet deep. When the remaining two ships of Columbus' expedition left Hispaniola, the route started in a manner that would've aimed them toward the Canary Islands, where they had taken on their last supplies before finding land in the New World. But, shortly after starting their original course, the ships suddenly made a 90-degree turn toward the north. That turn was made almost precisely over the Milwaukee Deep. Columbus had no way to know that he was over this feature, nor that it was part of an ocean trench. Had they continued on their original course, the ships would've gone over the entire Puerto Rico Trench — a notable area of seismic and volcanic activity.

The interesting point is that Columbus left Hispaniola, which is home to a mountain called Pico Duarte — the highest point in the Americas, east of the Rocky and Andes mountain ranges. Columbus' departure point was approximately halfway between the highest and lowest points. So, in an interesting parallel, Columbus' departure point for the return to Spain was symbolic of Jesus' departure point to return to Heaven. And, with no sonar, and no maps of the ocean bottom, how and why did Columbus suddenly change course to avoid the deepest spot in the entire Atlantic Ocean? With no knowledge of seismic history, how did he avoid an area where the Caribbean Plate and the North American Plate close in on each other to produce volcanic activity beneath the ocean? If the mission had been centered on the spice trade, would God have granted Columbus and his men such specific protections?

But, wait, there's more.

The Milwaukee Deep itself lies in between two points. Those two points, separated by hundreds of miles of ocean, have something quite remarkable in common. At a point off the western tip of Cuba, *and* at a point southwest of the Azores Islands, *both* at a depth of

---

[103] named for the USS *Milwaukee* (CL-5), a U.S. Navy *Omaha*-class cruiser, which discovered the Milwaukee Deep on 14 February 1939

approximately 2, 800 feet, are the remains of large, man-made structures. Canadian deep-sea explorer Paulina Zelitsky examined the structures off Cuba. They are monolithic in nature, just like Stonehenge and the statues on Easter Island. And, they display carved symbols of an unknown language. That language is remarkably similar to the writings of the Etruscans, a mysterious seafaring people that settled in the Tuscany region of Italy.

How did two (or three) ancient cultures develop similar writings and stone carvings, even when separated by such vast distances? How is it that such similar stone structures are found beneath the ocean — at the same depth — hundreds of miles apart? Could there really have been a place called Atlantis? (And, if not, then why is it called the *Atlantic* Ocean?) And, was Atlantis the capital of a global government?

And, what does all that have to do with Biblical prophecy? A lot.

Columbus claimed the New World in the name of Jesus Christ. The Bible says that, in the days of Noah, "the whole earth was filled with violence". (Genesis 6:13) The Hebrew word used is *Chamac*[104], which can also be translated "injustice". If there was a government of injustice and violence, then God could have dealt with it as He did with the Egyptians or the Jebusites or the Canaanites, right? There was no need to destroy the *entire* Earth — unless, of course, that violent and unjust government was *global*.

---

[104] Pronounced similarly to the name of the Arab terrorist group, Hamas.

As it was in the days of Noah, the world now has an organization that is trying to become a global government. That organization is, of course, the United Nations. But, is the UN violent and unjust? Consider these points from history. In its first major exercise of authority, the UN oversaw a war that stopped the advance of Communism on the Korean Peninsula. But, the UN did *not* drive the Communists back. Thus, the Korean people were divided. (During the rule of King Se-jong the Great, in 1433, the borders of Korea were pushed outward to their previous borders, which approximate the current border between China and North Korea.) So, while the United Nations had the opportunity to reunite the Korean people, and save the people of the North from oppression, the UN chose not to do that.

The same is true for Israel. After the establishment of the borders of the modern State of Israel, there was the question of the *Mizrahi*[105] Jews. They were the Jews living in foreign lands in the Middle East. In some cases, they lived in Jewish enclaves that had existed since the Babylonian Diaspora. They were citizens of the countries of their births, but some longed to migrate into Israel. After the founding of modern Israel, those other countries persecuted the *mizrahim*. Their homes, property, and businesses were confiscated. The treatment of the *mizrahim* at the hands of Muslim countries was quite similar in many regards to the treatment of European Jews at the hands of the Nazis. (That should be no surprise, given that one of Hitler's first foreign alliances was with the Muslim Brotherhood.)

---

[105] Hebrew for "Eastern". The plural noun version, "Easterners" is *mizrahim*.

When overseeing the enforcement of the Balfour Declaration and Israel's struggle for national survival, there was no UN support for the rights of the *mizrahim*. Several years ago, this writer pointed that out in a column[106]. To this day, there is no United Nations program to aid the *mizrahim* that are oppressed in the Muslim nations. (Oddly, there is a UN program purported to help them in Israel, where the United Nations considers them an "ethnic minority". Imagine that: Jews an "ethnic minority" in *Israel*[107].)

With these examples of geopolitical nitwittery in mind, remember that many people actually think of the United Nations as a legitimate global government, and not as a power-hungry, pro-Communist, anti-sovereignty monster. And, many of those same people see nothing wrong with the idea of a global government.

God, of course, sees it quite differently. He is King of the Universe, Creator of Heaven and Earth, and the sovereign Lord of All. Thus, the idea that He should be required to share some of His authority with the United Nations is ludicrous.

So, when there was a global government at the time of Noah, God caused a flood to destroy it. (That government apparently had its capital in Atlantis. Until the recent discoveries of the man-made, megalithic structures in the ocean depths, some people scoffed at the idea of a "lost continent" of Atlantis. The fact that the structures in the

---

[106] "Louder Than Words", Men's News Daily, 29 Dec 2003, click: http://mensnewsdaily.com/archive/k/kovach/03/kovach122903.htm

[107] And people want the UN to control the global environment?!

Atlantic and the Gulf of Mexico contain carved-stone hieroglyphs, and that those symbols resemble ones found in Assyria, Crete, Italy, and even Central America is *prima facie* evidence of a global language and culture.[108]) Despite knowledge of the flood, Noah's great-grandson, Nimrod, tried to start another global government. God, having promised to never again destroy the Earth with water, came down to Earth and divided the language of Nimrod's followers at the Tower of Babel. Now — just as the Bible predicts that a Third Temple will be built, and then house the Abomination of Desolation — there is a third global government. And, it looks as if the Son of God will be back soon to put down that one, as well.

But, wait, there's more.

Just as there was a Bible parallel in the significance of the departure point of Columbus from the New World, there is also significance in the location of the headquarters of the United Nations. And, the two are linked in a remarkable way. As this link is revealed, the reader will see that God truly does know the end from the beginning, and there is none like Him.

In order to understand the significance of the location of the UN Headquarters, we must first briefly examine the origins of the United Nations organization. The modern version was formed after the end of World War Two. But, that grew out of the League of Nations, which was formed after the end of World War One. The first organization

---

[108] For details, with graphics, see: "Update on Underwater Megalithic Structures near Western Cuba", *Ancient American* magazine, Nov 2001.

flopped, especially after its inability to prevent the conditions that led to World War Two. Some of those conditions included the famine and hyperinflation of the 1930s, as described earlier in this book.

During the period from the stock market crash of 1929 and the start of the FDR presidency in 1933, there arose an anti-globalist movement in the United States. One aspect of that movement was a group called The Farmers' Militia. At its height, there were 130,000 members nationwide! That would be a significant group now; but, remember that the population of the United States at that time was about half of what it is today. Thus, The Farmers' Militia had notable political power. And, they were not fond of globalist Franklin D. Roosevelt.

Partly because of the influence of The Farmers' Militia, and partly because of other pressures (including popular resistance to the introduction of the Social Security Number, which Roosevelt claimed "is not, nor will it ever be, a national identity number"), support for the League of Nations dwindled rapidly during the Great Depression.

The League of Nations had been founded in San Francisco. As we now know, that location is popular with globalist elites, who use it as a gateway to their secretive Bohemian Grove. As mentioned in the last chapter, those elites conduct pagan rituals before a large idol of an owl. Those pagan rituals bond the secretive global elites in a way that it difficult for "us normal folk" to comprehend. But, we must try to understand them, because those wealthy and powerful people control the society in which we live.

Global elites, in priestly robes, before owl idol at Bohemian Grove
Annual rituals occur during the Dog Days of Summer, marked by star.

Some modern people — sadly, including some Christians — might downplay the significance of the pagan rituals at the Idol of Lillith. Some might see it as a mere "farcical play" or some "fun and games". But, there are dire warnings in the Holy Bible regarding idol worship and the tolerance thereof. It is bad enough that our "leaders" do those things. But, it is even worse that our nation tolerates it. God does not. And, this author believes that God is poised to prove that very soon.

The proximity of the original League of Nations to the secretive Bohemian Grove should not be ignored. The global elites gather to discuss their plans, and to encourage one another. Bohemian Grove has been one of their primary gathering places for more than one hundred years. Thus, it should be no surprise that San Francisco was chosen as the headquarters for the original version of the framework for a modern global government.

But, wait, there's more.

Back in those days, some people saw the probable connection between the League of Nations and the Bible prophecy warning about the "whore of Babylon", which was a city built upon seven hills. (In our modern times, some people — who apparently conduct only a cursory reading of their Bible — have tried to label Senator Hillary Clinton as the "whore of Babylon". Although this author certainly understands how someone might think that, the Bible clearly states that the "whore of Babylon" is a *figurative* description of a *city*, and *not* a specific living woman.) Some people have tried to claim that the "whore of Babylon" is the Roman Catholic Church, because it is headquartered in Rome — a city founded upon seven hills. But, is that correct? Could there be another city that meets *all* of the elements of the description?

Yes. Buckle up.

Although the original League of Nations fell apart, and although it was founded in a city built upon seven hills, it was not the "whore of Babylon" ... *per se*. But, the rebirth of the League of Nations, in the form of the United Nations, does fit all of the elements of the Bible description of the "whore of Babylon".

Wait a minute! What does all of this have to do with the return voyage of Christopher Columbus?? Read on.

There is a little known fact about the history of Manhattan Island, the borough of New York City where the current UN Headquarters is located. As the population of New York City began to grow rapidly in the late 1800s, city engineers began working to <u>level the hills</u> of Manhattan Island. This was done to make it easy to build railroads — whether above or below ground — and for easier hauling of goods by horse-drawn wagons. The invention of dynamite made leveling the hills easier. This author was not able to find any precise information[109] regarding the size and number of hills. But, given the size of Manhattan Island itself, and a comparison to the surrounding terrain, it is not unreasonable to surmise that the island would've had about seven hills. (And, notably, the leveling of the hills began about 70 years[110] before the founding of UN Headquarters.) Without a pre-leveling map of Manhattan, it is impossible to document whether the home of the United Nations sits in a "city of seven hills". But, even if Manhattan did not originally have seven hills, it is known that San Francisco does have seven hills, and San Francisco was the home of the League of Nations that spawned the United Nations. Are there other facts about the United Nations Headquarters that fit the description in the final book of prophecy in the Holy Bible? Yes.

This author believes that the "whore of Babylon" is both the United Nations and the city in which it has its headquarters. That would mean New York City, and specifically Manhattan Island. By itself, the city

---

[109] Despite e-mail requests to the office of the City Engineer, and the office of the City Historian, with regard to records of the hill-leveling projects.

[110] The length of the captivity of Israel after its conquest by Babylon, which is also the name of a Long Island suburb of New York City.

has no authority to compel the "kings of the earth" to do anything. But, when coupled with the power of the United Nations — a power that those rulers gave to the UN in the first place — then the city becomes powerful. It is perceived as the capital of the whole world.

We first meet this powerful city called Babylon in Revelation 14:8. There, an angel declared that Babylon is "fallen, fallen". The city has been struck down because "she has made all the nations drink of the wine of the wrath of her fornication". The fact that she "has made all the nations" indicates that this new Babylon had *authority* over *all* the nations. Not since the ancient empires of Babylon, Persia, Greece, and Rome has any capital had authority over "all the nations" — until the founding of the United Nations in 1948.

The angel's declaration in Rev. 14:8 appears to be "out of sequence". But, if we recall that God and the Holy Bible are "outside of time", then that point becomes negligible. The *timing* of the destruction of the new Babylon is not as important as the *totality* of the destruction. It seems that God is giving a warning to his people. This is clearly stated in Revelation 18:4, where a voice from Heaven says, "Come out of her, my people...." The message here is that God will utterly destroy the city that has ruled over the nations, and that has caused the nations to become "drunk with the wine of her fornication". (Keep in mind that — during the early 1970s, when pornographic movies were becoming an economic force — New York proudly declared one of her nicknames to be "Sin City".)

When the destruction comes, it will be severe. That is why God warns His people to come out of that city. There will be no island of refuge within the city. Not only that, but God also warns in that verse "lest you share in her sins, and lest you receive of her plagues". What type of destruction might leave behind an opportunity for sins and plagues?

A massive flood, "as in the days of Noah".

But, unlike the flood of Noah's time, this flood will not cover the entire Earth. It will, however, destroy the entire headquarters that claims to hold authority over the entire Earth. And, as another angel declares in Revelation 18:10, "in one hour your judgment has come". There is no reference to "one hour" as being in Heaven, so it must be on Earth, where the city is located. What type of flood could destroy such a large city in a single hour?

A massive tidal wave.

And, now, we return to the significance of the voyage of Columbus.

That explorer, that "bearer of Christ", claimed the New World in the name of Jesus. But, when the United Nations rose up, it made a counter-claim for authority over the entire world. So, a judgment must be made. And, because God is the only true and righteous Judge over all of Heaven and Earth, that judgment must come from God, by way of Heaven, to the Earth. That judgment must be in a form that will be recognizable as having come from God.

There are two massive curves in the continental shelf of the United States coastline. Those two curves converge in a point, much like the point of the Pacific Plate that directed seismic energy toward the Kamchatka Peninsula after the Ivy Mike hydrogen bomb blast. (Thus, the opening of the sixth seal becomes a foretype of the destruction of the new Babylon, so that no one can say that God did not issue a clear warning to His people. But, how many modern Jews and Christians will heed the warning?) The convergence of those curves would funnel water directly toward ... yep, you guessed it, New York City.

So, if a massive stone is hurled to Earth from Heaven (as described in Revelation 8:8), and if that stone strikes in the Atlantic Ocean (let's say, for example, at the exact location of ancient Atlantis — the capital of the *first* global government ...), then the tsunami produced would be funneled directly toward the capital of the third (and last) global government. These patterns are not random. God knows the end from the beginning. Skeptics should consider the following points.

In order for this scenario to work, there would need to be a specific way to channel the energy of such a tsunami. Does such a way exist? Yes. At the edge of the continental shelf, there is a formation called the Hudson Canyon. It is a large groove in the shelf, and it is basically an undersea extension of the Hudson River Valley that runs into New York Harbor. And, the bottom of the Hudson Canyon leads to a large "empty" portion of the Atlantic Ocean that would be a perfect target for an asteroid to strike with minimal damage to other populated areas.

But, wait, there's more.

Draw a line north from the Milwaukee Deep to the island of Bermuda. That line forms the eastern side of the traditional boundary of the "Bermuda Triangle". (Some writers have developed other boundaries, based upon various analyses of the mysterious events in that area.[111]) Now, draw a line extending the west end of the *Atlantis* Fracture Zone (yep, that's its official name). Where those two lines intersect north-northwest of Bermuda is in that "perfect target" zone, at the northeast end of the Hatteras Plains, just off the low end of the Hudson Canyon, on the bottom of the Atlantic Ocean.

Now, draw another line from the Saints Peter and Paul Rocks (off the western coast of Africa) to New York City. Not only does that line cross over that same target zone, but it also runs approximately along the undersea Hudson Canyon. That second line, in this author's view, would be the ideal path for an incoming asteroid to produce a tsunami that would be funneled directly toward New York City. Further, because such an asteroid impact would be a "directional" event, it is possible that the track could produce a "burble" in its wake that would dissipate tsunami energy in directions other than in line with the trajectory of the asteroid. That final point would be totally in line with Revelation 18:4, which specifies that the damage is contained to the

---

[111] The name is in quotes, because the Office of the US Naval Historian (a repository of oceanographic information) does not recognize the "Bermuda Triangle" or the "Devil's Triangle" as an official name.

For a discussion about the difference between the "traditional" boundaries and the other boundaries of the "Bermuda Triangle", click: http://en.wikipedia.org/wiki/Bermuda_Triangle

city, and warns God's people to get out of this figurative Babylon "which reigns over the kings of the earth" (Revelation 17:18).

The headquarters building of the United Nations is very near the waterfront of Manhattan. (Only a highway — named after globalist President Franklin D. Roosevelt — separates the UN Headquarters from the East River.) As the tsunami approaches the shore of New York Harbor, and rises quickly to a massive height, the UN Building will be one of the first objects to be struck. Its flat shape will enable the wave's power to hit full-force at once. The destruction of the building will be nearly instantaneous. (For a fairly accurate depiction of what such a tsunami would look like, see the movie *The Day After Tomorrow*. Ironically, that movie encouraged the sort of Earth-worship that will invoke God's wrath. He is not mocked, and He uses even his enemies — such as Left-tilting Hollywood[112] — to fulfill His holy purposes. God is giving people every opportunity to repent and to worship Him alone. Will we pay attention?)

This author believes that, because of the size, speed, and trajectory of the incoming asteroid, the destruction will be channeled by the continental shelf and the ocean canyons in such a way as to leave most of the United States coastline intact. That is why Rev. 18:4 warns God's people to leave the *city*, but not the nation. So, not only will the destruction be a "signature of God", but so will the places that are *not* destroyed. And, because the ocean canyons were established long ago

---

[112] Even the name "Hollywood" has an evil hidden meaning. It is the type of wood used in the Druid sacrifices of humans.

(by the sedimentation after the flood of Noah), there will be no doubt that God's Word is holy and true.

It is only in recent times that sonar and submarine technology have enabled a few bold explorers to make discoveries such as the stone structures beneath the ocean. Those structures testify to the existence of an ancient culture with a common language. The fact that such similar structures are separated by hundreds of miles of ocean is evidence of a previous massive flood that destroyed a far-reaching civilization. The fact that such evidence matches the Holy Bible precisely should be further proof that the prophecies yet to be fulfilled are no less accurate than the historical record of those already past.

It seems that God somehow caused the return voyage of Columbus to suddenly turn north and avoid passing over the Milwaukee Deep for a specific reason. The Holy Bible makes clear that demonic forces reside beneath the earth. Could it be that Satan was planning to unleash the power of an undersea volcano, so that the rising hot gas crated a massive bubble that would destroy his expedition?[113] One of the stories that kept medieval mariners from sailing out of sight of the coasts of Europe and Africa was that of "churning cauldrons" and of "endless whirlpools" in the midst of the oceans. That would be a fairly accurate description of a bubble of volcanic gas, and its after-effect. (A bubble of hot volcanic gas — already large, even before expanding as it rises thousands of feet from the ocean bottom — could easily

---

[113] Scientists have explored this scenario as the likely source of ancient stories of sudden shipwrecks. The science behind it is demonstrated in the History Channel TV special titled "Rogue Waves".

become large enough to suddenly swallow a modern ship. The ships used by Columbus were only about the size of a modern house.)

The most ideal place for the impact of a large asteroid to produce a tsunami that would destroy New York City would be, interestingly enough, about in the center of the mysterious Bermuda Triangle. That area seems to also be approximately the location of the lost continent of Atlantis — about halfway between the two areas of undersea structures that were discovered.

Did the flood of Noah destroy Atlantis, and scatter portions of its buildings in different directions? And, when God caused the flood to recede, by sending it back into the "storehouses of the deep", was one of those storehouses located where the Milwaukee Deep is now charted? And, does that area hold some sort of Biblical significance? (To answer that question, see the graphic presentation of the cause of Noah's flood, from a scientific perspective, in the TV special series *Ancient Secrets of the Bible*, hosted by Charleton Heston. Perhaps it is no accident that he was stricken with Alzheimer's disease soon after that series was released. Satan does not like truth to be revealed.)

If the answers to the above questions are "yes", then it would make perfect sense for God to send an asteroid to the same place where the first global government had its capital, and to use the waters of the ocean named after that place to destroy the final global government of mankind. This is especially true when considering the essence of the events of the Sixth Seal, wherein sinful mankind used hydrogen — the most basic of all the chemical elements — to sow destruction. God will then use water, made from hydrogen, to cause mankind to reap the destruction that we have sown. And, just as an island was destroyed when the first hydrogen bomb exploded, an island will be destroyed when God uses water as a destructive weapon. He is not mocked.

It cannot be said often enough, especially in a study of prophecy: God knows the end from the beginning. Just as my series in The Crossbow has encouraged Jews and Christians to leave the "earthquake crescent" area of Northern California, this book now encourages Bible-believing Jews and Christians to get out of New York City.

That city is known as "the most Jewish city outside of Israel". Long lines of travelers fill the highways on many Friday evenings, as observant Jews seek to arrive at a Sabbath celebration before the sun sets. This is even more true when the Feast of Trumpets comes each year, and many NYC Jews head to the Catskill Mountain retreats for the weekend. (Traditionally, they must be indoors before sunset.)

If the above is true during normal times, imagine how much more important such travel will be as we approach The Tribulation. This author does not see a clear timeline for the asteroid impact. But, if the entire sequence of The Tribulation will be completed within the next seven years, then it would be wise for many to "escape from New York" as soon as possible. Those that wait will find it more difficult.

Just think: if the government schools had not spent at least a hundred years teaching falsehoods about the true reason for the explorations of Christopher Columbus, then perhaps mankind could have seen the warning signs sooner. But, then, the knowledge would not have been "sealed until the time of the end."

God forgive us and help us.

Chapter 4: Unfinished Business

This final chapter is being written on Monday, 11 August 2008. It will "finish up" some of the points presented earlier in this book. News events are lining up rapidly, and this information needs to get quickly into the hands of Bible-believing Christians, so that they can get about the business of witnessing for Jesus before it's too late. You will also see that God has "unfinished business" with Satan and his followers.

One point that needs more clarification is the analogy of the fig tree. The passage cited at the beginning of this book, Matthew 24:32-33, specifies that the fig tree's branch has become tender and put forth leaves. That means that the tree is mature enough to bear fruit.

The modern State of Israel has been called the allegorical fig tree. And, this book has shown that a complete Biblical "living" generation (60 years, versus the "power" generation of 40 years) has now lived in Israel. Therefore, it was only this past Spring — when the State of Israel had its 60th anniversary — that the tree had become mature.

Jesus said that, when the tree puts forth leaves in preparation to bear fruit, then you will know that Summer is near. As has been shown by several proofs, there is great reason to believe that Summer is the time when the prophesied events will begin. According to the Hebrew calendar, Summer ends when the harvest begins. That occurs shortly after the Festival of Trumpets. (This year, that festival comes on the 29th of September. And, the "harvest moon" is the 15th of September.)

In the Book of Revelation, there is exactly *one* event that comes in between the seventh seal and the first trumpet. That event comes after the silence in Heaven for "about half an hour". That event is the casting down of fire, taken from the altar of God by an angel, from Heaven to Earth. When that fire is cast down, it triggers the series of events (noises, thunderings, lightnings, fires, and an earthquake) that have been described in detail in this book as the California wildfires. The fact that it happened on the Summer Solstice should be further proof that Jesus meant every word very precisely when He gave us the signs of these times. He said that "it" is near, even at the door. Jesus described "it" in response to the disciples' questions about what would be the signs of "these things" (the End Times and The Tribulation) and of His return. Although no man knows the hour nor the day of Jesus' coming, we are *expected* to know the signs and seasons. And, we are expected to be watching in hope for them to occur.

Jesus cursed a particular fig tree, and it withered. But, even that tree had a purpose in God's plan. The purpose was to be an example of how Jesus' followers could ask God for anything via faithful prayer.

Some people think that it was "unfair" for Jesus to curse the tree, because "it was not the season for figs". But, as the Lord of all, He had the authority to do it. Moreover, there is another lesson to be learned from the fig tree.

If the tree that was cursed near Jerusalem represents the nation of Israel *at that time*, and if Israel has now been revived, then the lesson is two-fold. First, the love and mercy of God endure forever. And, if she will recognize the coming of her Messiah, then Israel can be forgiven. Seeking forgiveness is a sign of maturity. And, the fig tree has now become mature enough to bear fruit. Will it?

One of this author's great hopes is that, by showing the details of how God knows the end from the beginning, at least some of the people of Biblical Israel will come to recognize the visitation of their Messiah. And, having come to that recognition, they will then bear fruit for the Kingdom of God by telling others about Yeshua Ha' Meshiach. The writings of the Apostle Paul make clear that salvation comes first to the Jew, and then to the Gentile. Can a branch leave its tree behind? If not, then how can we Christians ignore outreach to true Israel?

This author believes that <u>the first trumpet of Revelation sounded on the Feast of Trumpets on the 29th of September 2008</u>.[114] This book has shown in clear, logical progression how all of the signs up to that point have *already* been fulfilled. (Indeed, the final sign of preparation was actually fulfilled *while* this book was being written.) There are also proofs from history, politics, geography, and linguistics to show that these signs <u>match *every* detail</u> of the predictions in Revelation.

Many years ago, this author became acquainted with a Jewish Christian. He explained the unique trials of that special group of people. His family held a funeral for him after he announced his faith in Yeshua Ha' Meshiach. They had nothing to do with him after that.

---

[114] In the **4th Edition** (Feb 2009), this paragraph was updated for tense.

But, now that the fig tree is mature, this author's hope is that it will bear fruit. If this book helps Bible-believing Jews to see that their Messiah has already come, <u>and is coming *back* soon</u>, then it will have achieved a major goal. And, that goal can only lead to more fruit for the Kingdom, and to better relations between Jews and Christians.

But, how can that goal be achieved if modern churches do not awaken to the deeper truths of Scripture? How can modern preachers, much less their parishioners, explain to the Jews the truths of a Jesus that they barely know? The book's other goal is to awaken Christians.

One of the sad truths of Scripture is that, instead of awakening, many Christians will fall away. They have nursed on "spiritual milk" for so long that they are unable to digest *any* spiritual meat. But, for those that ask, Jesus says that they will be given the Holy Spirit and wisdom. This book was not the result of any dreams[115], visions, or visitations. It is only the result of reading and seeing, seeking and finding. Let the reader do likewise, for the branch of the fig tree has become tender, the leaves have begun to shoot forth, and it is time to produce fruit.

the folly of ... folly

There is a bit of unfinished business regarding the story of Christopher Columbus. It is linked to the monolithic structures found on the ocean floor. It is also linked to the fairly recent discovery of a vast oil supply beneath the bottom of the eastern Gulf of Mexico, in the international

---

[115] The prophetic dream mentioned in a prior chapter happened in early 1995. That dream helped this author with understanding the total scenario (especially Matthew 25:41). But, that dream was *not* the basis for this book.

waters between Florida and Cuba. That supply was discovered when a test well, called "Jack-2", was drilled a couple of years ago. The oil supply at the Jack-2 site is believed to be one of the largest discovered in North America. (And, we could sure use it right now.)[116]

Undersea explorers have mapped the location of the remains of the *USS Maine*, the warship whose sinking near Cuba sparked the Spanish-American War in 1897. Many historians suspect that newspaper magnate William Randolph Hearst may have paid someone to plant a bomb aboard the *Maine*, thus fulfilling his famous boast, "If you want a war, I'll give you a war."

The location of the *Maine* is not far from the Jack-2 site. Notably, it seems that neither the Democratic nor the Republican members of Congress are pushing for undersea oil exploration near Jack-2. Instead, the Democrats seem intent to stop all American oil drilling, and the Republicans seem intent on drilling only in Alaska. Is there a reason why nobody seems to care about the vast oil supply beneath the international waters in the Gulf of Mexico?

Two concepts come to mind. One has to do with the wreckage of the *Maine*. If the undersea evidence proves that an American sailor (or reporter) did plant a bomb aboard the ship, then the entire Spanish-American War becomes a historical *faux-pas* at best. Spain's loss of its Philippine Islands colony is called into question, because that loss came as a result of losing the war to the United States. This author is not skilled in international law, but it seems reasonable to wonder

---

[116] More about the influence of petroleum in the Afterword of this book.

whether Spain would have any legal claims with regard to the war being started by an act of American sabotage *against America*.[117] (Could the planned North American Union, supported wholeheartedly by President Bush, be a way of *repaying* Spain "by stealth" for its losses in a needless and artificially-created war?)

The second concept has to do with the results of undersea exploration. Is it possible that American submarines (or, subs from other nations) have discovered *more* remains of the lost civilization of Atlantis? Could it be that such archaeological remains confirm the Bible account of Noah's flood? And, if so, then are there other things that are also proven by remains under the ocean? What is at the bottom of the Milwaukee Deep? Does the ocean bottom contain the evidence of enormous amounts of water returning to the "storehouses of the deep"? (For example, are there any whirlpool-shaped formations etched into the stone of the undersea mountains?) And, if so, then what effects might those discoveries have upon American foreign relations — especially with the Muslim nations that hope to discredit the Bible (as Turkey tried to do regarding the site of Noah's Ark), because they intend to undermine and destroy Israel?

More germane to the purposes of this book, what might the evidence of a previous global government — proven to have been destroyed by

---

[117] That concept gave rise to the Top Secret plans of the never-implemented Operation NORTHWOODS in 1962. The plans were declassified in 1997. They revealed that American military generals had cooked up a scheme to conduct <u>acts of terrorism within the United States, against Americans</u>, in order to "gin up" public sentiment for a full-scale invasion of Communist Cuba and the toppling of its president-for-life, Fidel Castro.

God — do with regard to public sentiments about the United Nations? And, how long ago might such a discovery have been made? (Was it classified Top Secret?) Are there any technologies that can be gleaned from the archaeological records of an Atlantian civilization? And, if so, then are any of those technologies being examined by American scientists right now? And, if so, are those technologies for good or evil? (Legend has it that an advanced Atlantis had developed a "death ray" that harnessed the power of the sun — focusing it much like a modern laser.) Are any such ancient records being used to develop modern, high-tech, military projects such as the HAARP in Alaska?[118] Has mankind tinkered with our environment — especially the weather[119] — to the point that Earth is truly out of balance?

These questions lead to other questions. Why would educated voters re-elect a purportedly "conservative" American president that thinks the Constitution is merely "a God-d---ed piece of paper"? Why would pastors encourage their congregations to vote for a president that cares little about the border security of his own country? How could a sitting president allow several Border Patrol agents to be sentenced to prison for ... securing our borders? Is this what the Bible meant when it said that "strong delusion" would come over the people?

---

[118] One of the documented functions of the High-Energy Atmospheric Auroral Research Project is "tactical and strategic weather control". That was documented, via a FOIA request, at least as far back as 1994.

[119] In an apparent Freudian slip, President George W. Bush once referred to Hurricane Katrina (Sep 2005) as "a very powerful weapon".

Shortly before this chapter was started, news reports appeared that Mexico has just passed an "anti-homophobia" law. It is now a *crime* in Mexico (as it became in Canada, two years ago) to say anything negative about the condition of homosexuality! Back in 1994, during a debate while running for Congress, this author was accused by a college-age audience member of having "homophobia". I quickly responded, "I do not have homophobia. I have homo-*nausea*!" And, I am repulsed by homosexuality because ... God is. (There is a long list of "sins" in the Bible, and a short list of "abominations". The most oft-mentioned abomination is homosexuality. It is an offense to God, because it is a total repudiation of His design of the human body — in His own image — and of His design for the beauty of sex. The word "abomination" means "something that is loathsome or hated".)

President Bush wants to form a North American Union, in which the United States will merge with Canada and Mexico. If it is already illegal in those two surrounding countries to say anything negative about homosexuality, and if President Bush has no regard for the tenets of our Constitution (such as free speech), and if he currently has more than 20 working groups planning to "harmonize" the laws of the three countries[120], then how much longer will it be before this "conservative, Christian" president enables the government to imprison Christians for speaking out against sinful and loathsome acts such as homosexuality?

---

[120] That fact is thoroughly documented in the book *The Late, Great USA* by Dr. Jerome R. Corsi, and in several of his columns for *WorldNetDaily*.

Our country, and our world, have gotten to this point — at which condemning an abomination is considered a crime, even if it is not in the law books (yet!) — largely because Christians have been too wimpy to take a stand. And, unfortunately, they have largely become so because they have been *taught* to be that way by their pastors!

Another goal of this book is to encourage Christians to engage in a deeper study of the Holy Bible for themselves. The logic is two-fold. First, as a wise Russian Orthodox priest once told me, "God has no grandchildren." In other words, we are all responsible directly to God for our relationship with Him. On Judgment Day, it won't matter what one's husband or pastor or president did; it will only matter what you did. The Holy Bible is now available in more languages than at any point in the history of mankind. Here in the United States, a person can purchase a Bible almost anywhere — even from the book department of some large grocery stores. So, there is no excuse for not getting to know God better by studying His Word. If you were standing before God, and He asked, "Why didn't you study my 'love letter to you' better," then it would be no excuse to answer, "My preacher didn't tell me that I'd have homework during the week."

The second reason is more practical, and gets to the logical result of the events of The Tribulation that is now in progress.[121] If congregations of Christians are put under persecution, then there will be dispersion of believers. It took years for the Nazis to round up the Jews, and they never did get all of them. (Sadly, the taxpayers of the

---

[121] In the **4th Edition** (Feb 2009), this sentence was updated for tense.

United States have paid to develop technology that the Nazis had only dreamed of. That technology will be used to hunt down some of those very taxpayers. Back in the early 1990s, members of the Militia Movement tried to warn us, but the media branded them as "kooks".) If churches are dispersed by persecution, then who will teach and preach the Word of God to hungry souls? Yep, you and I will need to. Are you up to the task? If not, then you need to study your Bible.

If the concept of The Tribulation starting in only a few weeks from the release of this book is not enough to spark your interest, then "neither will they believe if someone were to rise from the dead". We were warned "politically" 15 years ago[122] by the Militia Movement, but few paid attention. This book is an attempt to warn people "religiously" of many of the same things. And, there are far more signs in place now than before. Will people pay attention now?

But, why would people pay attention now, when so many people have ignored signs that have been right in front of their faces for so many years leading up to this point? Let's examine another sign.

---

[122] Remember that, in His mercy, God granted King Hezekiah 15 more years of life. What did he do with it? He fathered the most evil king in Israelite history: Manasseh. And, he showed the Temple treasures to emissaries from an enemy nation. That led to Hezekiah's captivity and death.

What have we done with our extra 15 years? We re-elected Bill Clinton, and then elected and re-elected another president (Bush-2) that had equal concern (none) for the authority of the Constitution. And, we have now elected another occupant of the White House that is intent on destroying America with his infectuous Socialism. (In the **4th Edition**, Feb 2009, the preceding sentence was updated for tense.) Remember that, on the Hebrew calendar, Bill Clinton and Barack Obama were born on the same date, 15 years apart. Hmmmm. Does anyone still doubt the hand of God in these events?

One of the clearest warning signs in all of the Holy Bible is the "mark of the beast". Even when revealing the meaning of the mark, the Book of Revelation contains an immediate clarification. "Here is wisdom. Let him who has understanding calculate the number of the beast, for it is the number of a man: His number is 666." (Revelation 13:18)

American voters have, in recent years, elected men that had clear intentions *against* America. And, it seems that "we" have elected[123] a man whose anti-American sentiments are even clearer than those of Presidents Bush, Clinton, and Bush. Every one of those presidents used American military power, without a Constitutionally-required declaration of war, to bring our country down via needless fighting and spending. Clinton also used American military might directly against American citizens (near Waco, Texas, in April of 1993).[124]

Our folly is not limited to the election of presidents. We have elected, and continue to re-elect, candidates for the House of Representatives and the Senate that are also dedicated anti-Americans. Nowhere is this more true than in electing members of the Progressive Caucus. When I ran for Congress the first time (1994, NY-26), the incumbent

---

[123] In the **4th Edition** (Feb 2009), this sentence was updated for tense.

[124] If anyone still thinks that the Clinton-Reno raid upon the Mount Carmel campus was a "law enforcement operation", then they should consider the following questions. Why did military personnel participate in that "civilian" operation? Why were Psychological Warfare troops and technology used against the people inside? Why did the agents/troops smash the buildings, bury the evidence, and then burn the rubble? And, most importantly, why did they kill *all* of the people that they purportedly intended to "rescue"?

(Maurice Hinchey) was a leading member of that Communist group. When I tried to expose him, voters — especially those of Ukrainian descent (Hinchey is an ethnic Ukrainian) — scoffed at me.

About a month before the release of this book, Congresswoman Maxine Waters threatened the president of Shell Oil Company, during a now-famous hearing about the price of gasoline. She threatened him with *socialization* of the oil industry! (Waters is also a member of the Progressive Caucus, which is the Congressional arm of the Democratic Socialists of America. Look it up yourself.) Even the "lamestream" news media was taken aback. When the firestorm of public opinion burned against Maxine Waters, her defender was Maurice Hinchey.

A wise and veteran writer and activist, Joan Battey, told me in 1994, "You cannot pull the voting lever for a conservative with one hand while reaching for a government handout with the other hand." That is the essence of the folly of the modern American voter. We have become conditioned — largely by the government-run schools — to *expect* the government to "rob from the rich, and give to the poor". And, we have become conditioned to view *ourselves* as poor, in order to qualify for a government handout. Thus, we use our cars (with air conditioning and automatic transmissions, of course), our computers, our cell phones, our fax machines, and our Internet access to tell the government just how *poor* we are, to qualify for welfare! What folly!

Just what did the Branch Davidians learn from their Bible studies that the government does not want us to know? Has some of that information now been "unsealed" by God, 15 years later?

And, now, the folly of electing Communists is coming home to haunt us. The membership of the United States House of Representatives is now 15 percent comprised of members of the Progressive Caucus! (When I first ran in 1994, that number was "only" ten percent. Why would Americans elect even *one* Communist to lead our government?) So, should it surprise anyone that our Congress has put restrictions on our own oil industry, while increasing oil imports from our enemies? Should it surprise anyone that Chinese agents can go into the library of the United States Patent Office and obtain invention ideas, thanks to the 1996 "patent reform" laws sponsored by Maurice Hinchey? (He has also made trips to Cuba to encourage better United States relations with that Communist country.) Should it surprise anyone that our teachers can no longer make progress teaching, because they are so bogged down by the paperwork requirements of the "No Child Left Behind" laws pushed by President Bush? (If it comes as a surprise to you that a "conservative" president would push un-Constitutional legislation, then you simply haven't been paying attention.) When he used the power of the Federal government to push that bill, he should've been impeached for abusing the power of his office. (But, why would a Congress that let him remain in office after starting a war without a declaration worry about a little detail such as abusing power? We have been conditioned — by government-run schools — to think of a Federal takeover of local education as a "good" thing.)

The above examples are only a few highlights. America is in danger. And, if we are the example for the world of a "Christian nation", then the whole world is in danger. And, if we voted for the conditions described above (and "we" did — even if "you and I" did not), then we are responsible for the outcomes. And, if we voted for Communists, and if Communism is anti-God at its core (and it *is*), then we deserve the wrath of an angry God. And, that is the folly of voting for those that "tickle the ears" with their big-government promises of wealth redistribution (which comes directly from *The Communist Manifesto*).

And, <u>now</u>, you are ready to understand the number of a man's name.

Just as the signs of America's decline toward Communism have been all around us for a long time, so have the signs of a leader that has dedicated his life to bringing about that decline. But, whenever a few of us tried to warn America just how dangerous Bill Clinton truly is, we were mocked as "extremists" for simply pointing out the facts. Here is a set of facts that I have tried to tell people for ... 15 years.

the number of the name

I believe that Bill Clinton is still the main candidate for The Antichrist.

The reason for the use of the term "main candidate" is that history is full of people that could have become The Antichrist. For various reasons, those other people did not get the job.[125] But, as this book has shown, the time is now ripe for the appearance of The Antichrist.

---

[125] That point, which has been touched upon earlier in this book, could be the subject of a book-length discussion of its own. The bottom line is that three men signed the 1993 Oslo Peace Accords that have undermined the security of Israel. And, the other two are dead.

In 1994, a man used a phrase to describe the abuses of power that were happening under President Clinton. He told me, "They're breaking the law, in the name of the law." That summed it up well. Logically, it doesn't make sense; yet, that was exactly what was happening. It was confusing. And, God is not the author of confusion. Clinton himself, describing the Tax Code he signed, said, "The Devil is in the details."

The era of the Clinton presidency — and, indeed, his entire life of public office — can be summed up in a word: lawlessness. The law became a weapon, to be used against his political enemies. One of the clearest examples was when the IRS was assigned to "audit" a church that had taken out full-page ads during the election. The ads said, "A vote for Bill Clinton is a sin against God." Then, the ads compared Clinton's political stances against Scripture. And, the ads were right. But, truth was no defense against the IRS agents that demanded not only the financial records of the church, but also the records of every member of the Church at Pierce Creek, just outside of Binghamton, New York. I was not a member there, but I did attend quite a few Sunday evening services (having attended my own church on Lord's Day mornings). And, it was not enough when the IRS got the doors shut at the Pierce Creek location. After the church bought a new building in downtown Binghamton, and reopened as The Landmark Church, the IRS continued to harass the congregation until that church was also shut down. But, unlike the group near Waco, at least the Clintonistas allowed Pastor Dan Little and his congregation to live.

This book is about religion, and not politics. But, we cannot discuss what is happening in these politically-charged times without looking at the political situations that got us to these times. My first talk-radio program was called PR² (which is pronounced "PR-Squared"), because it was about Politics and Religion. It was a double-play on words, because the show aired from the campus radio station of the State University of New York at Binghamton, which has a renowned engineering school, where "πR^2" was in everyday usage.[126] In the introduction to each program, I would explain that every major aspect of our lives is affected by "politics and religion"; so, people need to discuss them openly (thus, countering the populist mantra that good folk should "never discuss politics and religion in public"). Just as my radio program openly mingled politics and religion, this book shows that — even if people put their heads in the sand — those two things will still have major influence over their lives. So, it is best to become well-informed on those topics. But, when we become well-informed, then we are responsible for our decisions. That scares some people so much that they think they can avoid responsibility by means of an especially virulent form of willfully blissful ignorance. They can't.

Avoiding truths does not make them untrue.

And, creating a simplistic lie does not make it into a simple truth. For example, during the conservative boon of President Ronald Reagan's administration, some people tried to twist the simple truth of Revelation 13:18 into something that it was not. The New King James Version uses modern numerals to represent the number of the beast.

---

[126] The campus is also a bastion of Commie-Liberalism, which is why my conservative talk-radio show was featured on the "Family News in Focus" broadcast on Friday, 24 December 1993.

Verbally, people often say, "Six-six-six." But, that is misleading. Older translations spell it out clearly, such as "six hundred and sixty-six", or "six hundred, three-score, and six". This detail is important, to avoid confusion.[127] Some evil people, taking easy advantage of the dumbing-down of America by government-run schools (especially regarding matters of the Holy Bible, which is banned by those schools), tried to claim that President Reagan's name "proved" that he was The Antichrist. How so? There were six letters in each of his three names: Ronald Wilson Reagan. Therefore, using the erroneous "six-six-six" formula, the political Left confused some people into thinking that Reagan could be The Antichrist. Although he was certainly not perfect (nor is anyone), Reagan was the last "real" president this country has had. He was definitely *not* The Antichrist.

So, why do I believe that Bill Clinton is? Read on.

The Bible describes The Antichrist as the "man of lawlessness". In 1992, we citizens of the United States elected a president that: claimed that he "didn't inhale" while smoking marijuana in college, dodged the draft during a war, wrote that he loathes the military[128], protested against our country — in a foreign country — during time of war, knowingly associated with Communist officials — in a foreign country — during time of war, used his Arkansas governor's security

---

[127] There's that word, again. God is not the author of confusion.

[128] But, as the president, he did not loathe the use of cruise missiles, nor the propping up of a Socialist dictator in Haiti, nor sending our troops to protect the Muslim Bosnians as they continued their thousand-year Balkan War against the Christians of that region.

detail to procure women with which to have illicit sexual affairs, had at least one other illicit sexual affair after he was elected president, committed multiple acts of perjury to cover up his lawless acts, tried to suborn others to commit perjury on his behalf, and is suspected of being at least tacitly involved in the deaths of dozens of people that had first-hand information about his illegal activities. It certainly seems to this author that Bill Clinton is a politician with more in common with Stalin than Gandhi. Clinton is a man of lawlessness.

But, wait, there's more.

Revelation makes it very clear that The Antichrist will have a name that is clearly identified with the number "six hundred and sixty-six". There have been many formulas used to compare many names to that infamous number. But, what did Jesus say about that number? The answer, technically, is "nothing". But, something that Jesus said about life in general is surprisingly applicable to calculating the number of the name of The Antichrist. "Let the little children come to Me, and do not forbid them: for of such is the kingdom of God. Assuredly, I say to you, whoever does not receive the kingdom of God as a little child will not enter it." (Mark 10:14-15) The lesson here is not merely to allow little children to openly express their faith in God. The lesson is also that, if we have faith in our heart, then even the deep things of God will be as simple to perceive as the basic things that a little child can perceive. Put another way, "It's as plain as the nose on your face."

So, is there a plain and simple formula for Bill Clinton's name, to prove that he is a likely candidate to become The Antichrist? Yes.

> # A, B, C, D...
> # 1, 2, 3, 4...

The preceding text in the box shows the simplest form of cryptogram in the English language. Letters are given a numeric value, in the same order as the alphabet. So, how does that add up in this case?

WILLIAM JEFFERSON BLYTHE CLINTON

Many people forget that President Bill Clinton was not born with that name. His birth name was Blythe. His birth father was killed in a car accident when Bill was two years old. Bill's mother remarried, and Bill's mother added the stepfather's last name. If we add up the letters in his *full* name, the total is ... six hundred and seventy-two. But, wait.

Bill Clinton did not use his birth last name; but, it was not negated. The name Blythe was simply "in the background", so to speak. So, let's take another look.

WILLIAM JEFFERSON ~~BLYTHE~~ CLINTON

If we subtract one for each letter of the crossed-out name, the remainder is 666. The scoffer might say, "That's too simple. Where is the 'signature of God' in that?" Read on.

Bill Clinton won the presidency in large part by support from Leftist women and from college students. Both groups are known for their support of abortion. Anti-abortion activists often refer to abortion by the term "the slaughter of the innocents". That term was originally used to describe the slaughter of the Hebrew children in Egypt by the Pharaoh — who feared the prophecy that a Deliverer of Israel had been born. By the time he learned of the prophecy's fulfillment, Moses was two years old. So, Pharaoh ordered his soldiers to kill all Hebrew boys aged two years or less. (Of course, Pharaoh had no idea that The Deliverer was living in his own house!) The lament of the Hebrew parents came to be called "Rachel weeping for her children".

In like manner, by the time that King Herod of Israel had learned from the Wise Men that The Messiah had been born in Bethlehem, the event was two years old. Like his counterpart, Herod ordered the slaughter of all boys aged two years or less. That event was also called "the slaughter of the innocents". And...

In the Greek language, the prefix "anti-" is normally translated as "opposite". But, it can also mean "rival" or "substitute". Whenever The Antichrist appears, he will not only institute a global reign, but he will do so by substituting a new faith in him for people's faith in God. In order to achieve that, The Antichrist will mock or twist as many of the aspects of the life of Jesus as possible.

Whereas the parents of the innocents lost their children when they were two years old, this child lost his parent when he was two. Whereas there is a historical stigma against being "fatherless", the story of Bill Clinton's loss of his father endeared him to some voters. Jesus taught, "A disciple is not above his teacher...." (Matthew 10:24) But, when he had just recently graduated from law school, Bill Clinton was elected as the attorney general of Arkansas. Jesus taught, "...whoever desires to be great among you, let him be your servant." (Matthew 20:26) But, Clinton refused to serve in the military.

Then, there is the question of "The Bill Clinton Body Count". The reporter that originated that list has never been sued by Clinton. It would seem that Clinton, a lawyer, is following the legal doctrine that "silence equals acquiescence". Put plainly, if Clinton had basis for a lawsuit regarding the body count list, then he would have filed it.

And, then, of course, there are the White House scandals. Even the list of "-gates"[129] is so long as to almost seem repetitious. Hillary Clinton spontaneously coined the term "bimbo eruptions" to describe reports of Bill Clinton's numerous sexual dalliances with various women. (He used his Arkansas State Trooper security detail to hunt for women to have sex with during and after official state functions, when he was

---

[129] The suffix "-gate" evolved from the 1972 scandal that centered around the break-in at the Watergate Building by the team nicknamed the "White House plumbers". Their job was to "fix the leak" caused by Daniel Ellsberg, a former Defense Department employee that leaked large amounts of highly-classified information to the *New York Times* during the Vietnam War. Ellsberg's book was called The Pentagon Papers, and it was an intelligence coup for the Communists. But, for all the information published, there were hundreds of pages of Top Secret information that were *not* published. The team of "plumbers" broke into the office of Ellsberg's psychiatrist, in an attempt to find out what Ellsberg had done with the rest of the information. The team of "plumbers" was led by the enigmatic G. Gordon Liddy, who spent five years in Federal prison for refusing to testify to Congress. Upon release from prison, Liddy became a very successful talk-radio host.

governor of that state. (The famous White House affair with young intern Monica Lewinsky *was* public business, because Clinton delayed meetings with foreign decision-makers to have sex with her.) The most serious Clinton scandal (that we know of) was Chinagate, in which Clinton greased through the release of sensitive satellite communications and navigation technology — developed by the Loral Corporation under a project called Iridium. The technology was given to the Communist Chinese government, by Loral, in a blatant *quid pro quo* for a $600,000 donation by Bernard Schwartz — president of Loral — to the Democratic National Committee during the time leading up to Clinton's 1996 re-election campaign.[130] That technology made it possible for China to catch up to America in two important military applications, both based on the processing of information from Global Positioning System (GPS) satellites. Those two areas were missile targeting and hand-held locators. The first enabled China to accurately target individual *buildings* within the United States, for ICBM strikes. The second enabled their spies and military special operators to have the same GPS capabilities as our own. In the eyes of many in this country, Clinton committed treason and deserved the death penalty. Instead, he was re-elected. (And, shortly after that, he "accidentally" bombed the Chinese embassy in Serbia, killing the person believed responsible for brokering the technology exchange. The paper trail died with him, and Clinton was never prosecuted.)

Those are just the major highlights.

---

[130] For a concise report on the details, see an article by Charles Smith, "Loral:

There is a large and detailed book, *Compromised — Clinton, Bush, and the CIA*, by Terry Reed, that details the drug-running operations at the remote Mena Airport in northwestern Arkansas. Those operations were connected to the Iran-Contra arms-shipment operations[131] (Reed was the CIA pilot that trained the Nicaraguan *contra* pilots to airdrop the shipments.) Agents of the "off-book" operation were documented, by Reed, bringing back large amounts of cocaine from Panama[132] after refueling there on the return leg of the arms-drop flights. Reed's book alleges that Clinton's financial advisor made large deposits to Clinton's bank account after those cocaine-laden flights returned to Mena. That was apparently part of the "rent" package for use of the airport. In return, Clinton provided a secure perimeter around the airport, via a special unit of the Arkansas State Troopers. The first two names on the Bill Clinton Body Count list were 12-year-old boys playing along the railroad tracks near the Mena Airport. As were many deaths on that list, it was ruled a suicide by the Arkansas Medical Examiner's

---

going to the Schwartz side", *WorldNetDaily*, 01 March 2000, at: http://www.worldnetdaily.com/index.php?pageId=7090

[131] At the height of my military career, I was approached by a former Green Beret to join the team of "kickers" aboard those Fat Lady missions. The name comes from the C-123 Provider aircraft used for the larger shipments. For personal reasons, I declined the invitation. Later, the Fat Lady was shot down over Nicaragua. The only survivor was Eugene Hassenfus, a kicker that had always worn his own parachute rig. He spent six months in a Nicaraguan prison, where he gave an interview to *60 Minutes* and told all.

[132] Several of my columns have detailed the corrupt actions of the man that was the base commander at my last military assignment. Military tradition is that a commander, or his close representative, should greet an aircrew that comes back from certain types of missions. At that base, I worked on security patrols, on the flightline, almost every night. The only time that I saw that particular commander come out to greet a returning overseas transport aircraft was if it was coming from Panama. Hmmmmm.

Office. The peculiar nature of those deaths coined the word "Arkancide". The last time I checked, there were 57 names listed.

Now if that's not Antichrist material, then I don't know what is.

But, wait, there's more.

Several writers have pointed out that Barack Obama's given names are from the Arabic language, and that both his birth father and his stepfather are Muslim. A few have even shared the definitions of those two names. (Barack = "blessing"; Hussein = "handsome") But, not even Dr. Jerome Corsi, in his thoroughly researched book *The Obama Nation*, has revealed the meaning of his last name. One of my recent columns in The Crossbow did that. Obama's last name means "crooked".

Yes, you read correctly.

That discovery has been confirmed by two African-born professors of African linguistics, one of whom is from Kenya and is a native Luo[133] speaker. That professor went even further, explaining that prophetic

---

[133] Luo people live mainly in southwestern Kenya. Their language is spoken by only 13 percent of that country's population. Contrary to popular myth, Obama's family was fairly well off financially. They are also involved in national politics. Barack Hussein Obama II went to Kenya and personally campaigned for the election of a Muslim man (his cousin, Raila Odinga) that ordered the deaths of large numbers of Christians that did not vote for him. Churches were burned with their congregations *still inside*. Yet, in the face of all evidence to the contrary, Obama calls himself a Christian.

Notably, southwestern Kenya also has some of Africa's highest concentration of AIDS patients. There, it's called "trucker's disease", because promiscuous sexual contact at truck stops rapidly spread AIDS across the continent.

meanings are used in name selection, and that many African tribes do not utilize the Western concept of a "family name". Therefore, even one's last name is "given" by the parents. (In the case of the Obama family, they have adopted the Western tradition of a family last name for the last three generations. That decision is believed to have been politically motivated.) The language professor explained to me that the name Obama is most often given to a child born with crooked legs, which is considered a very bad omen. So, as my column[134] revealed, African diplomats would read his name as meaning "the blessing from the handsome one that is crooked"; and, they would view it negatively.

But, wait, there's more.

The record of lies surrounding Barack Obama seems to top even that of Bill Clinton. One of the most central is the "bodyguard of lies" that surrounds the circumstances of Obama's birth. There have now been two proven forgeries of his birth certificate released to the public by the Obama campaign. After two researchers pointed out that the graphic pattern of the paper — especially the fancy border — was not consistent with samples known to have been issued by the State of Hawaii, then his campaign released another certificate. That one turned out to have a faint impression of his *sister's* name in the scanned image of the paper.

---

[134] "Obama name shocker: 'crooked'", 24 July 2008, The Crossbow; republished by Renew America.

The following day, I discussed that "revelation" on-air with Dr. Corsi when he was a guest on The G. Gordon Liddy Show. The topic was the release of *The Obama Nation*, which climbed to the top of the Amazon sales charts during the course of that guest interview.

Many people have focused on the fact that, if Barack Hussein Obama turns out not to be a natural-born citizen of the United States, then he would not be eligible to run for president. But, the problem goes further. If he was not a citizen (he has never been naturalized, and his birth certificate is questionable) when he ran for the United States Senate, then his entire term in the Senate has been fraudulent. And, in turn, that would mean that his Senate seat (and back salary!) would belong to his 2002 rival. That person is Dr. Alan Keyes, who also ran for president.[135] (The news media almost totally ignores Keyes, claiming that Obama was "*the* Black candidate for president". That is another skewed "fact". Barack Obama is half White, and at least half of the remaining half of his ancestry is Arab. So, at most, Obama is only one-fourth Black.[136]) The very foundation of Obama's political existence seems to be based upon an enormous lie. Why?

Perhaps he was literally born for that purpose.

As described earlier in this book, Barack Obama and Bill Clinton share the same birthdate (the 22nd of Av) on the Hebrew calendar. Hebrew tradition puts emphasis on the birthdates of prophets.[137] The Bible

---

[135] In the **4th Edition** (Feb 2009), this portion was updated for tense. To learn more about Alan Keyes, click: www.AIPnews.com

[136] And, if only one-fourth of Blacks supported him, then he would've lost!

[137] The greatest example thereof is the birth of Jesus. Unlike the common tradition, evidence points to Jesus' birth as having actually been at Passover. That would make him the greatest prophet of Israel, and would confirm Him as The Messiah. I pointed out this fact in "Christmas needs an extreme makeover", published 26 Dec 2005 by Renew America. (NOTE for 3rd Edition: Some Messianic believers think that Jesus was conceived at Hanukkah, and born during the Feast of Tabernacles. Since there is no dated

makes a strong link between The Beast and The False Prophet. In the mind of a traditional Hebrew scholar, their having the same birthdate would be strong evidence of God's signature on that link.

This author has believed from the start of Bill Clinton's inaugural speech (which was, in part, a New Age sermon[138]) that he was the man that would become The Antichrist. The details of his rise to power, and the details of his presidency (including the Flight 800 coverup, which I've helped to investigate) only serve to underscore that belief. But, in order to become The Antichrist, there would need to be a False Prophet that appoints The Beast to a high political position, from which The Beast[139] then *becomes* The Antichrist.[140] The simplest

---

record of Jesus' birth, any assessment of a date is based upon interpretation of Scripture. I respectfully disagree with those other believers, but admit that no one knows the answer this side of Heaven. The date of Jesus' birth should not be a bone of contention. Instead, the main focus of Christian believers should be the imitation of Christ and the blessed hope of His return to establish the Kingdom of God.)

[138] An examination of those details would provide enough material for a series of columns. But, current events are moving so fast that there is little time for an intellectual exercise in retrospection. The opening line of Clinton's speech, on 20 Jan 1993, said that by that ceremony "we force the Spring". That drew cheers from the New Agers in the crowd, and was a reference to the pagan Feast of the Invincible Sun (the worship of Baal). It was from that feast that Saturnalia arose in ancient Rome. That was the day each year on which more Christians were killed than any other. Hmmmm.

[139] For more about the hidden meaning of that term, see my column, "The beasts of the earth", published 03 July 2007 by Renew America. Many believe that Bill Clinton is actually a descendant — whether by natural means, or by some laboratory action — of the Nephilim, which is why he will not release his medical records to the news media. His genes don't fit us.

[140] The two are the same person. But, he does not "officially" become The Antichrist until his bodily indwelling by Satan. That occurs three days after a fatal head wound. More about that shortly.

scenario is that Barack Obama will be elected president[141], and then he will appoint Bill Clinton to be the next American ambassador to the United Nations. Once there, Clinton has enough supporters to be elected as the next Secretary General. That would, in effect, make him "king of the world" — exactly as the Holy Bible predicts will happen for The Antichrist. The closest similar opportunity in history was when Hitler and Stalin signed a secret pact to mutually support the Socialist goals that each espoused. (Of course, that required enormous bloodshed, as will the Socialist goals of the Clinton-Obama agenda.) Hitler and Stalin only *appeared* to be enemies. In reality, their views were so similar that a pact between them was almost inevitable. That same appearance of conflict marked this year's Democratic primary races. But, now, Clinton has openly supported Obama for president — even while Senator Hillary Clinton *is still* a candidate for that office!

And, that leads us to....

Shakespeare wrote, "Hell hath no fury like a woman scorned." Documented news accounts reported that Hillary threw things (including a lamp) at Bill during their frequent marital arguments in the residential portion of The White House. But, if you think that she was angry over the "bimbo eruptions" and the "cookie recipe", imagine how angry she must be over Bill's formal endorsement of Obama!

---

[141] And, the technology is in place to "make it happen", regardless of how people vote at the polls in November. (<u>Added note for the 3rd Edition</u>: the election results were exactly as predicted. It is no small factor that Fox News recorded video of the Black Panthers intimidating voters in Pennsylvania with a nightstick as they approached the polling place. Police are already

Hillary Clinton is not a woman with whom one should trifle. Many people (this author included) still hold a personal belief — despite official reports to the contrary — that White House chief counsel Vince Foster was murdered. The person with the most to gain from the silence of Foster was Hillary Clinton. Not only did Foster know "where the bodies were buried" with regard to the Clintons' financial dealings, the mass firings in the White House travel office, the "pogrom" when all of the United States Attorneys were fired by President Bill Clinton in a single day, the number and nature of Bill's sexual dalliances, but ... there were also published news accounts of eyewitnesses that saw Foster and Hillary in compromising positions at various times and places.

Some people believe that several people on the Clinton Body Count list were put there by decisions from Hillary, and not Bill. This author believes that there is a strong parallel between the final scene of Vince Foster's life and the opening scene of the 1976 Sean Connery movie *The Next Man.* In that scene, an oil executive looks forward to a romantic meeting with his mistress. The two enjoy a scenic drive, dinner, drinks, and then go to a fancy hotel room. Then, while the man is in the shower, the mistress puts a sedative in his champagne. He drinks the champagne, and then they have sex. He falls asleep after, and she smothers him by means of a plastic bag over his head. She then calmly cleans up the crime scene, changes her hair color, and returns to her pampered high-society life in England. Unknown to her

---

gearing up for riots, and that scenario could reappear in December, when the Electoral College convenes to cast the votes that *really* elect a president.)

wealthy family, she is a professional assassin. Does anyone else see a strong set of parallels there?

And, that leads to....

There is one person that can, and routinely does, get past all of the security checkpoints that surround even a US president — whether current or former. That person is his wife. And, in the case of a sitting US senator and now a Cabinet officer[142], Hillary Clinton has even more ways to get through security than most other presidential wives.

My personal (political, but not necessarily prophetic) read on the situation is that she will not do the "obvious" in a fit of envy. Instead, my guess is that she will actually get a position within the Obama administration. The most likely spot would be attorney general, where she could do at least as much damage to the United States as did Janet Reno, the attorney general that served Hillary's husband.[143]

Hillary has been riding Bill's coattails for decades, pursuing political power. But, now that they have reached the zenith of their power, Bill has endorsed someone else for Hillary's ultimate prize. Nonetheless, she could do far worse than becoming America's lawyer-in-chief.

---

[142] That's right: current. Hillary Clinton "suspended" her candidacy, but she did not fully "withdraw" her candidacy — even after Bill endorsed Obama. (In the **4th Edition**, Feb 2009, this portion was updated for tense and new information. Hillary Clinton has now been confirmed by the Senate as the new secretary of state under Obama. As a member of the Cabinet, it will now be even easier for her to pass through security.)

[143] This paragraph was intentionally left intact during the 4th Edition update, to show another prediction that came true (at least, partly). Many insider political pundits also expected Hillary to become the attorney general.

Once she has established herself in that position, and come to the realization that she can never go any higher, then she will not need Bill any more. If that scenario pans out, and if Bill gets caught in another bimbo eruption, then a vase flying across the room (or "accidentally" falling from a bedroom window — see Judges 9:53) could ostensibly solve Hillary's "problem", while also fulfilling Bible prophecy.

Regardless of how the details work out, the Bible predicts that The Antichrist will be revealed to mankind after the person that is The Beast receives a fatal head wound, and then rises from death after three days.[144] All that this presentation shows is that there are three people currently in positions of political power that also fit all of the details necessary to become The False Prophet, The Beast, and the person that kills The Beast and thus changes him into The Antichrist. And, the person that does the killing would have "opportunity, means, and motive" to commit the murder. Hmm, an "unholy trinity" indeed.

The Apostle Paul wrote in 2nd Thessalonians 2:3 that the day of the return of Jesus will not come until a great falling away comes first. Then, the "man of sin" is revealed. This book has shown that a great falling away has recently occurred within Christianity. And, this book has just revealed the precise ways in which Bill Clinton fits the mold for The Antichrist and that Barack Obama will likely be elected into a position that would be necessary for the job of The False Prophet. But, does Obama "fit the mold" of the person in that job? Read on.

---

[144] Thus fulfilling the "rival" definition of the prefix "anti-" regarding Christ.

The cited chapter uses four terms: "the man of sin", "the man of lawlessness", "the son of perdition", and "the lawless one". Many scholars believe that all four terms refer to the same person. But, what if they don't? What if two of those terms are synonymous with The Beast, and the other two are synonymous with The False Prophet? (This question does not in any way change most existing views of this section of prophecy. It is only presented because of a detailed examination of that prophecy in light of current political events.) This author believes that "the man of sin" and the "son of perdition" refer to The False Prophet, and "the man of lawlessness" and "the lawless one" refer to The Beast. And, here is how they refer to Obama and Clinton.

The word "perdition" means "the condition of being lost". All people are "of sin", in that we have a sinful human nature. But, what does it mean to be both "of sin" and "of perdition"? The answer is contained in that same chapter. The man that bears that title "opposes and exalts himself above all that is called God or that is worshipped, so that he sits as God in the temple of God, showing himself that he is God."

Have you noticed that Barack Obama is setting himself up to be regarded as a political figure "of Biblical proportions"? Some joke that he is The Messiah, while others seem to seriously believe that. Obama claims to be a Christian, although he was raised a Muslim. The key here is that, although he has recently repeated his claim to be a Christian, <u>he has *never renounced* Islam</u>.[145]

---

[145] That point was confirmed on the final day of editing this manuscript (Mon, 18 Aug 2008) in an on-air chat with Dr. Jerome Corsi. He was the

So, while many gullible Christian voters will assume that he is a Christian — despite his very anti-Christian views about abortion, homosexuality, Socialism, the so-called Black Gospel[146], and an all-encompassing government — devout Muslims see Obama as simply practicing *taqiy'ya*[147] at a very sophisticated level. That is why the terrorist group Hamas gave a formal endorsement to the Obama presidential campaign. Yet, millions of Americans still support him.

If, instead, Obama had renounced Islam, then there would be constant death threats against him. Why? Because, when a Muslim publicly leaves that religion, true Muslims believe it is their duty to punish the apostate by death. (Compare that to the Christian version, spelled out in Hebrews 6:6, in which God inflicts a punishment that no person could ever equal.) <u>There have been no death threats against Obama by devout Muslims, because *they* believe that he is *still* a Muslim.</u>[148]

Sadly, there are too many mamby-pamby Christians that fall for the deception that God the Father (whose formal name is Yehowah) is

---

guest, and I was a caller, on Nashville's live and local Michael DelGiorno talk-radio program (on SuperTalk FM 99.7, WWTN).

[146] which is Communism masked in terms that appeal to Black people that do not study their Bibles very well. (If they did, then they would *never* follow a preacher that stands at the pulpit asking God to damn their own country.)

[147] The Muslim practice of routinely deceiving non-Muslims. The Qur'an teaches that such deception is not only acceptable, but is a necessary aspect of daily living for true Muslims. Non-Muslims are to be deceived regarding the intentions of those bringing Islam into a non-Islamic country, until the Muslims become strong enough to take over the government. Sadly, here in America, it appears that a forcible takeover will not be necessary. Instead, people will vote for the masters that will enslave them.

[148] This point was also confirmed in the on-air chat with Dr. Corsi.

somehow the same as Allah, the god of the Muslims. Even some Muslims believe that lie. But, the true Muslims would never accept such a concept. (If they did, then why would they constantly declare that Jews and Christians should be killed? If we all believed in the same god, then we would be their brothers. We definitely are not.)

Obama is taking considerable advantage of the dumbing-down of modern Christianity. Wimpy people that claim to "go to church" (as though that automatically meant that one knows Yeshua Ha' Meshiach as their Savior) cannot figure out the difference between "discernment" and "judgment". Therefore, they poke their heads in the sand with regard to discerning the truth that God and Allah cannot be the same. They say, "Judge not," and think they are being "good Christians". What a surprise when Yeshua says to them on Judgment Day, "Depart from Me, for I never knew you." How could He know them, given that they refused to know Him? And, if people refuse to study their Bible enough to know Jesus (Yeshua) from Allah, then they are fair game for a deceiver to come along and lead them astray.

Once the deception has placed Obama into power, he can complete it by integrating political power with religious power. I believe that, if Obama is elected president, then he will help to usher in *shari'a*[149] as the law of American government. There might be sparse resistance, which might compel him to make the change piecemeal, but *shari'a* seems to be the goal. There was a hidden code in his campaign-trail

---

[149] Islamic religious law, which includes the requirements for women to wear the *burka*, the requirement for society to come to a halt five times per day for prayer to Allah in the direction of Mecca, and the killing of non-Muslims.

reference to visiting "57 states, with plans for a 58th". Reporters claimed that it was a slip of the tongue, caused by fatigue. Hogwash! There are 57 member countries in the Organization of Islamic States. Thus, if he forces *shari'a* upon the American population, <u>then *we* will become the 58th Islamic state</u>! Is that the type of "change" you want?

more unfinished business

While doing Bible study for this final chapter, I came to a realization that has never hit me in all these decades of study. And, it shows that God truly does know "the end from the beginning". And, it proves the truth of the Scripture in which He declares, "Vengeance is mine." (Deuteronomy 32:25)

The entire third chapter of the Book of Daniel is devoted to the story of the three young men — Shadrach, Meshach, and Abed-Nego[150] — who resisted the king's order to bow down and worship an idol of himself. There is more to the story than some realize. The king of Babylon, Nebuchadnezzar, was ruler of an empire that covered the entire known world of his day. He was, in effect, a global ruler. (He did not rule the entire planet. But, he did rule as much of the planet as he knew about.) When his government reached its zenith, he decided that he should be worshipped in the form of a gold idol.

The story is widely known, even among those that do not believe in the God of the Bible. The Three Holy Youths refused to serve the gods of Babylon, or to bow down and worship the idol of the king. So,

---

[150] In the Orthodox Church, they are called The Three Holy Youths.

he had them thrown into a fiery furnace. But, they did not die. Not only did they live, but also their clothing did not even smell of smoke! And, while they were inside the furnace, the king saw a fourth man inside the furnace with them. He declared that the fourth man "is like the Son of God". (And, it was the pre-incarnate Jesus.)

Now, here is the unfinished business.

Revelation 20:10 describes a terrible scene in which the devil is cast into the lake of fire and brimstone (burning sulphur). He is cast into it, "... where the beast and the false prophet are. And, they will be tormented day and night forever and ever." Do you see the parallel?

The False Prophet causes people to worship The Beast. The False Prophet gives an image of The Beast the power to speak.[151] Then, The Beast causes all to worship that idol, or to face death. And, to "cement the deal", The Beast causes all people that do worship his idol to receive a mark in their right hand or their forehead. Anyone that does not worship the idol does not get the mark. Anyone that does not get the mark cannot buy food. Thus, only by compulsion, The Beast will experience the "worship" of the entire world ... except true Christians.

But, it won't last long. And, at the end, the people that followed the bad example of Nebuchadnezzar will then experience the punishment that Nebuchadnezzar had designed for the followers of the One True

---

[151] New note for the 4th Edition. The government is pushing to mandate digital television (DT). The original conversion date was Wed, 18 Feb 2009. On that date, Obama "just happened" to also sign his first law into effect. For more details on the significance of these facts, see the Afterword.

God. Thus, in the end, Satan, The Beast, and The False Prophet will be thrown into an eternal equivalent of the fiery furnace of Babylon!

But, those that resist them will enter into the eternal rest prepared for the saints. They will be able to eat of fruit that is continually fresh — because the trees will bring forth fruit once per *month*, instead of once per year. (Revelation 22:2) That fruit will bring "the healing of nations". Thus, there will be no more war. All things will be made new; there will be no death, no lying, no sorrow, no curse. (The curse, from Genesis, was that man would "eat by the sweat of your brow".)

As the time of The Tribulation draws near, the choices — for God, or against God — will become increasingly clear. At first, there will be some degree of confusion — especially after the events that follow the sounding of the first trumpet. On one hand, many will see it for what it really is, and will choose to follow Jesus. On the other hand, those that already hate God in their hearts will look for a way to actually blame Christians for *causing* global catastrophes. As the battle lines become drawn, the choices will be made clearer, culminating in a time when The Antichrist attempts to force everyone to accept The Mark of the Beast. By that time, there will no longer be any room for doubt, because implantation of The Mark of the Beast will be associated with the worship of the idol of his image. (Astoundingly, some people have *already* implanted micro-chips into their newborn *babies*! Some of those parents were actually gullible enough to think that the *only* reason for The Chip was so that the government could "help" them if their child is ever kidnapped. Putting a microchip into one's baby is the ultimate form of child abuse.)

Society is being conditioned for accepting The Mark in a variety of ways. One of those ways is by watching "reality" TV shows. Has anyone else realized there is very little *reality* behind the concepts of those programs? Instead, they should be called "humiliation TV", because the real goal of the program is to see just how much the contestants will humiliate themselves in order to get the prize. (The only such program that had any level of reality — *Combat Missions*, on the USA Network — was cancelled after only half a season.)

If people will eat a bucket of worms, or allow themselves to be covered with tarantulas, or live in a house with people that they cannot stand, or ask someone to marry them — all while having every detail recorded for broadcast — just to win a cash prize, then there is no doubt that many people will accept The Mark when told that the alternative is that they will not be able to buy groceries ever again. And, if millions of people will plant themselves in front of a TV to watch those exercises in self-humiliation, then there is no doubt that society will someday find it entertaining to watch "blood sports" where Christians are forced to fight each other to the death, or be fed to the lions, or tortured into accepting The Mark or continuing the torture until death. If you don't think that this is possible, then explain the popularity of the "reality" program American Gladiators, or the even more popular professional "wrestling" — where gore earns more.

And, society was conditioned to watch those as "entertainment" by decades of watching professional football. (Coach Vince Lombardi, the idol of many football fan-atics, famously said, "Football is the moral equivalent of war.") And, society was conditioned to view professional football as legitimate entertainment after years of government-run schools teaching young boys that getting paid to play games is a legitimate "career" choice! Do you see a pattern there?

How many preachers have cut their sermons short, or even changed the schedule of church services, so that congregations could watch a football game or other sporting event? Who is king at that church?

How many preachers have encouraged their parishioners to frequent, or have even held church meetings at, Starbucks Coffee? What difference does that make, you ask? Have you ever wondered about that peculiar picture on the label of every Starbucks product and store?

Lillitu – "Queen of the Night" (ca. 1950 BC)
Photo of the "Burney Relief", a terracotta image from Babylon
(Image source: Wikimedia Commons)

The above image of the demon-goddess Lillith is remarkable for many reasons. For starters, note that the pose, and even the items in her hand, are exactly the same as the "woman" depicted on the Starbucks company logo. That is no accident. Starbucks is one of the most "gay-friendly" companies there is. Lillith promotes sexual deviance.

Note, also, the fact that Lillith is flanked by owls — the mascot of the Bohemian Club, which owns the Bohemian Grove. Again, that is no accident. Lulled to sleep by decades of television brain-mush and government-run school "education"[152], modern Christians think that idol worship is some faraway concept that only mud-people act upon. And, that dumbed-down state of Christianity is exactly what the idol worshippers have wanted for the past two thousand years! Just who handed it to them? Preachers and parents!

Were there some preachers that have encouraged their congregants to put microchips into their babies? I don't know. But, given the sad state of modern Christianity, I would not be surprised. There have certainly been preachers that have encouraged their congregants to make purchases at Starbucks, because I've heard them with my own ears! And, who would be surprised, when the preacher of a large "church" tells his congregation, "God damn America," and they cheer for him! And, then, that church produces a major candidate for

---

[152] If there seems to be a pattern of criticism against government-run schools, you are correct. As a teenager, this author was an unwitting guinea pig for a program called Outcome-Based Education. It was developed by a handful of teachers — who sold the program (printed by graphic-arts students, at school expense), at tremendous profit, to other school districts. The address of the building where OBE was developed: **666** Reynolds Road. Really.

president! So, don't be surprised if some "churches" tell their members that accepting The Mark is a good idea. (Some might even try to use Scripture to justify it, even as candidate Barack Obama tried to use the Sermon on the Mount to justify his support for homosexuality!)

With the above information in mind, perhaps some readers — that have read this book with a skeptical eye — will now see that the idea of modern business and political leaders worshipping an idol of an owl, and making their political decisions based upon the "guidance" that they receive at the Bohemian Grove, is not as far-fetched as it might have seemed a couple of chapters ago.

Indeed, another major factor in our modern government is also based upon a form of idol worship. That factor is abortion. In ancient times, rulers solidified their cruel version of political power by expecting subjects to sacrifice their children to the demon-idol Molech (sometimes also spelled Moloch). The difference between modern abortion and ancient ceremonies to Molech is that the modern participants don't even get the spiritual "benefit" of believing that they are killing their children for the greater good of society. (Or, do they? Some government-run schools teach so much about over-population that students probably internalize the concept as a spiritual notion.) At some point, in some secret place, I am confident that some members of the abortion "industry" do, in fact, offer up the remains of aborted babies to the demon Molech. Investigators have found piles of burned fetal remains in remote locations. Was it a case of avoiding the payment of proper disposal fees, or was it demon worship? Or, both?

The Tribulation will be a difficult time, as many Christians wake up to the realities presented in this book. But, for those that get beyond their comfort zone, and begin to understand the reality behind why it is called a church "service"[153], there will be eternal rewards. Ask God for wisdom and the Holy Spirit. Learn to see through spiritual eyes. Read your Bible as though it is what it really is — both an instruction manual for daily life, and a combat manual for spiritual warfare. Learn to worship God "in spirit and in truth". And ... *pray*!

There are four things that Christians are *commanded* to pray.
1. Pray for the peace of Jerusalem.
2. Pray that your flight will not be in winter, or on the Sabbath. (Matthew 24:20[154])
3. Pray for your brothers and sisters in Christ — especially those under persecution and captivity.
4. Pray for your nation — especially the leaders, that they may have wisdom, so that we may live peaceful lives in all godliness and tranquility.

---

[153] We serve God with our *time* and our talent, as well as our treasure. And, yes, there are also parallels between serving God and military service.

In many countries with a long Christian history, a one-hour church service would be regarded as ridiculously *short*. Most modern Americans need to develop far more of a "servant's heart".

[154] In the year 2012, the first full day of winter (22 December) falls on a Saturday — the Jewish Sabbath.

If all of the other observations and calculations of this book are correct, then that will also be the *first* Saturnalia *after* The Antichrist is revealed. I believe that the true Christians will be "raptured out" before then. (See 2nd Thess. 2:6-8 for an explanation of the timing relationship between the withdrawal of the Holy Spirit and the revelation of The Antichrist.) But, for those that are *suspected* of being Christians, their troubles are really beginning at that point.

Note that there is no Scripture reference for most of those commands. All of them are in the Holy Bible. The reader is hereby encouraged to look them up for yourself. Get to know your Bible, as a Marine knows his rifle. Keep in mind that, when Jesus was directly confronted by Satan in the wilderness, Jesus began every reply with, "It is written..." Can we do better than our Lord Jesus?

Imagine the changes that can come if millions of people will "humble themselves and pray" — especially following the above commands, and the pattern of The Lord's Prayer. The changes will not necessarily be outward. <u>We cannot stop The Tribulation from happening, as some might suppose</u>. God planned it long ago; it is His will. Instead, the changes will be within us and in our relationship with God.

Those are changes that matter. Those are changes with eternal rewards. Remember that, "The Kingdom of God is within you". Remember that, during The Tribulation, there will be some that will have "the seal of God" for protection from those that will hunt them.[155] Remember that, even if you are not among "the elect", your eternal reward is guaranteed if your name is written in The Lamb's Book of Life. Remember that Jesus told His disciples not to rejoice because demons were subject to them, but to "rejoice instead because your names are written in heaven".

---

[155] Revelation clearly states that "the elect" 144,000 people will come *only* from the 12 tribes of Israel. (That negates the beliefs of some sects, which teach that they are the replacement for Biblical Israel.) This author's personal belief is that the elect will come from the membership of the group Jews for Jesus. It is my understanding that their membership is approaching 144,000.

Remember that you, too, can be assured that your name will be written in heaven. How? Get to know the *real* Jesus (not that wimpy version that is described in those wimpy churches that give money to idols). Read your Bible! Pray! And, ask God to give you wisdom and the Holy Spirit. Then, learning to take up "the whole armor of God", ask God to give you salvation through the sacrifice of His Son, Our Lord and Savior Jesus the Christ. And, then, rejoice! Again, I say, *rejoice*!

That decision could cost you. Friends on earth might abandon you. (But, you will gain "ten thousand times ten thousand" new brothers and sisters.) Society might mock you. (Hey, they also mocked the Wright Brothers.) If you belong to one of those wimpy churches, they might reject you (just as the synagogue of Capernaum rejected Jesus.) The government might hunt you. (But, that season won't last long, even if they catch you.) But, don't worry, because I've read The Book, and we win in the end.

Even so, come Lord Jesus.

Afterword

As the final chapter of this book was being typed, computer problems were in plentiful supply. Just as a mighty storm came in an attempt to prevent Jesus from arriving at the shore of Gadara, and thus casting out the legion of demons from a man there, it seems that The Enemy was trying to prevent this book from warning and encouraging people regarding the truth of the Holy Bible and the authority of Jesus. (Ponder this question: if Gadara was located in *Israel*, then why were the Gadarenes raising *pigs* in the first place?! Now do you understand why there was an entire *legion* of demons there?)

Also while this chapter was being typed, the Republic of Georgia has invaded the tiny country of South Ossetia. In retaliation, Russia sent tanks and troops, and damaged the Georgian capital of Tbilisi. What does this have to do with Bible prophecy? Plenty.

Russia was the last Christian empire, before Communism took over. After the Communist-led government of the Soviet Union fell apart, and the Russian Republic replaced it, several of the former Soviet "satellite republics" broke away. Georgia was one of those. But, the Georgian possession of South Ossetia wants to rejoin with Russia.

The above might seem to be merely an internal ethnic struggle. And, were it not for the massive and strategic oil pipeline that passes through the Caucasus Mountains of that region, it might remain so.

But...

An American lobbyist formerly worked for the Republic of Georgia. He was instrumental in the negotiations to get the pipeline into that region. And, that pipeline has the ability to undermine the economy of certain Muslim nations to the east. As Russia seeks a return to its former nationalistic pride (which included a strong Christian heritage), and the Muslims seek to destroy or undermine Christianity by means of their oil profits, the pipeline becomes an important trigger in the sometimes delicate world of international relations.

Many claim that Russia is the ancient "Gog and Magog" mentioned in several End Times prophecies. Regardless of whether that identity is correct, it is obvious that the largest country on the planet (by land area; China is the largest by population) would certainly figure into any End Times scenario. And, if the Russian oil pipeline can supply oil faster and cheaper than shipping it through the Persian Gulf, then that pipeline can easily become a source of controversy that could trigger a war between Russia and any number of Muslim countries.

Oddly enough, that scenario could put the United States into the role of "bad guy". How? We currently have oil trade established with those Muslim countries — even though several of them consider us to be their enemy. The need for oil in America could force us to side with the Muslims against Russia. (That becomes even more likely if Barack Obama becomes president.) But, before you get all excited and think that you can prevent this cataclysmic clash by simply voting for "the other guy", consider this fact.

The lobbyist that negotiated the deal for the Georgia pipeline is now the foreign-policy advisor to the presidential campaign of ... Senator John McCain! (And, *his* last name means "son of Cain". Consider the Biblical implications of that.)

There is some degree of speculation about whether Senator McCain is eligible to run for president, based upon his place of birth. (I made the mistake of doing some of that speculation in a column earlier this year. It was the only time that I've caught flack for any inaccuracy in my writings.) I tend to view the speculation about McCain's birthplace in the same way as speculation about McCain's alleged "collaboration with the enemy" during and after his captivity in Hoa Lo Prison during the Vietnam War. Both sets of accusations are based upon "facts" that have poor documentation at best. (I followed the trail through the "paper jungle" regarding McCain's time in Vietnam. Some of the most widely-believed documents "supporting" the allegations turned out to be very good counterfeits.) So, although I do not trust John McCain politically, I am not ready to put him in the same boat with Obama.[156]

On Thursday, 21 August 2008, a lawsuit was filed in Federal court in Philadelphia. That lawsuit was significant enough to force this book into a second edition — in order to include these two paragraphs — only a few days after the first edition was released. The lawsuit, notably, was filed by a Democratic Party insider that is loyal to Hillary Clinton. He claims that the suit was filed to protect the Democratic

---

[156] The above was written in the 1st Edition of this book. See the Update Notes later in this Afterword for information that came out late in the election cycle, and thus after the original release of this book.

Party from any damage caused by Barack Obama running for president while he in ineligible for that office! On page 5 of that lawsuit, in Paragraphs 17 and 18, plaintiff Phillip Berg alleges that Obama was born in Kenya! If that is proven to be true, then not only is Obama not eligible to run for president, but he was also ineligible to run for the US Senate four years prior. And, that would mean that Obama's seat in the Senate rightfully belongs to his 2004 rival, Dr. Alan Keyes.

The fact that Keyes is a champion of conservative Christian issues, while Obama is a champion of Socialist issues of poor moral basis, and that both men are running for president now, and that both men ran against each other for the same Senate seat four years ago, seems to this writer to be more than mere coincidence. Perhaps another way that God has put his "signature" on 2008 as the start of The Tribulation is by having two men of such utter contrast available for the voters to choose. Perhaps this is a test by God upon the voting public. Hmmm.

Update Notes

The 3rd Edition was released on Wednesday, 05 November 2008, the day after the election of Barack Obama. **No changes were made to the Obama-related content of the book.** Footnotes were expanded to underscore the accuracy of this book's original predictions. And, one paragraph was edited to correct an error regarding the Hebrew feasts. An astute Messianic reader in the Saint Louis area reported that error.

The 4th Edition was released on Monday, 23 February 2009, to update the fact that (as predicted) Obama did take the White House and he did appoint Hillary Clinton to a Cabinet office. The 4ᵗʰ Edition also changed certain sentences from future tense to past tense, to reflect the post-inaugural informaton. The text has been updated to add the spelling of the Arabic word *Filistin*, which my research found is the correct word that is wrongly translated "Palestinian" in English (to hide the true nature of their terrorism). And, certain typographical and grammatical errors, not caught in previous editions, have now been corrected.

The government push for digital television (DT) carries with it huge implications for society and for our freedom of expression. Among other things, DT makes it possible to insert "alternative reality" (AR) technology into the picture with a much higher degree of realism. The best-known example of AR is the insertion of the yellow and blue lines onto the telecast of a football field. Players appear to run over the lines, which appear to be painted upon the field. The colored lines are digitally inserted between the players' legs and the grass.

Now that AR has been around for a few years, it has advanced to the point that "seamless" video alterations can be done in real time. For example, anti-government protesters could demand to have their concerns aired in a live TV-news broadcast. They could demand to see the telecast on a monitor at the protest location, to ensure that they are really getting their message out to the public. And, those demands could be met. But, the public might see — modified in *real time* — images of those same people saying and doing things other than what is really happening. (Jesus predicted that, even if we were to "see" false christs, we are not to go out after them and their phony "miracles".)

In a worst-case scenario, an oppressive and anit-Christian government could actually capture and torture Christian protesters — on live TV-news broadcasts. Even if the Christians remain true to the end, the TV could show altered images of those same people accepting The Mark and swearing allegiance to the False Prophet and to The Beast.

If you doubt that the above could happen, consider this. An illegal alien has been (ostensibly) elected to the office of president of the United States. Although he claims to be a Christian, he is still proud to recite (in flawless Arabic) prayers to Allah. But, he also carries a gold Hindu idol in his pocket for "luck"[157]. His very first act of signing a bill into law (the so-called "economic stimulus package") was done away from the White House at a ceremony in Denver. Why there? During his campaign, he was "worshiped" there by his Democratic supporters in a ceremony that even members of the Leftist news media commented had religious tones. Denver has the highest elevation of any state capital. Thus, Obama was "worshiped" again, in the "high place", when he signed a law that made him the provider of many people's daily bread. The Bible says that the False Prophet and/or The Antichrist, "opposes and exalts himself above

---

[157] The word "luck" comes from the word Lucifer. So, every time that a Christian wishes "good luck" upon another Christian, that person is actually (even if unwittingly) proclaiming "Lucifer is good". If you don't believe that, then why do you think that gamblers rely so heavily upon "luck"? If we truly believe that God is in control, then why would we say *anything* other than "God bless you" about someone's future plans? (Along a similar line, the custom of saying "God bless you" when someone sneezes comes from the pagan belief that one sneezes one's soul momentarily out of one's body. So, to prevent demonic possession, *pagans* pronounce blessings after sneezes! In other words, modern Christians have been so duped by "popular culture" that we offer God's blessings when we should not, and offer Lucifer's "blessings" upon fellow Christians when they need God's blessings! No wonder that Jesus needs to bring an army to fix things.

all that is called God or that is worshiped, so that he sits as God in the temple of God, showing himself that he is God." Obama has placed himself above all major religions (Christianity, Judaism, Islam, Hinduism) by the above actions. But, wait, there's more.

Remember that a true Muslim considers himself a slave of Allah. (The word "Muslim" means slave, or bondservant.) Remember that Allah is the moon-god of Mesopotamia. (The symbol of Islam is a crescent moon for a reason.) Remember that true Islamists (terrorists) plan their events around certain dates, and that dates which fall upon a crescent moon have the highest spiritual value to a Muslim.

According to the moon-phase calculator of the United States Naval Observatory, here is a picture of the phase of the moon at the exact time (noon, Eastern Time) that Obama took the inaugural oath.

Here is the phase of the moon at noon Mountain Time on the 18th of February, when Obama signed his first law at the "high place" in Denver.

The date for the mandatory introduction of digital television was moved. It was originally supposed to have been on 18 February, the same date when Obama signed his first law. Remember that, almost immediately after was inaugurated, Obama told the Congress that he expected to have an economic stimulus package passed and sent to him for signature "by Presidents' Day". Presidents' Day is one of the "Monday holidays" set by the Federal government. Why did Obama specify that day — a day when Congress is normally *not* in session? Did he have some plan in mind that would've required Alternate Reality television? Did his plan have some religious significance? Why a date that coincides with the crescent moon?

The ancient Hindus believe that their calendar was begun on a specific date, <u>which corresponds to the **18th of February** 3102 BC</u>. They believe that is the beginning of the "First Age", which they call Kali Yuga. Keep in mind that the Hindu goddess Kali is the queen of destruction. We saw a reference to the Hindu "destroyer of worlds" in the quote by nuclear scientist Robert Oppenheimer after he unleashed nuclear destruction upon the world. Remember that Obama keeps a Hindu idol in his pocket. Remember that the two men (the False Prophet and The Beast, who will later become The Antichrist) that cooperate with Satan are part of his plan for destruction. Mere coincidence?

The day when digital television is now scheduled to become mandatory (Fri, 12 June 2009) is not a crescent moon. But, just a few days later, at midnight on the 17th of June, there will be a crescent moon. Is there now an "adjusted" plan to use DT and AR to provide altered television images of some worldwide event? What will happen at about that time?

The 14ᵗʰ of May (on the Gregorian calendar) is the anniversary of the founding of the modern State of Israel. (On the Hebrew calendar, the anniversary is the 5ᵗʰ of Iyyar, which in 2009 equates to the 29ᵗʰ of April — thus, another high-probability date for a terror attack.) Although Obama did not appoint Bill Clinton to become the US ambassador to the UN Headquarters in New York, there are still other United States missions to United Nations offices in key locations. They include the European Union (EU) headquarters in Brussels, Belgium[158]; the Vatican, and the Israeli Knesset in Tel Avia. Any one of those posts would put Bill Clinton in a position to influence world events. (And, he could still be promoted later to the New York headquarters.) Given the penchant of globalists and Islamists for tying key events to specific dates from history, and to certain astronomical events (the crescent moon being high on their list), it seems to this writer that the start of mandatory digital television is planned so that some world-changing event can be broadcast to the public in an "altered reality" form.

Predictive Notes: It is notable that Obama has moved with dramatic speed to effect the "change" upon which he campaigned for president. Is he on a timetable? Does he realize that the Bible has a timetable of its own. Does he have some sort of guidance that "time is running out" for Socialists and other God-haters to force their version of "change" upon our country and upon our world?

On the Hebrew calendar, the 9ᵗʰ of Av is associated with destructive events. In 2009, the 9ᵗʰ of Av corresponds to the 30ᵗʰ of July. Look for a destructive event on that day. Look for a date with false spiritual

---

[158] There is a supercomputer there with the nickname "The Beast".

significance on the 7th of July. That date corresponds to the 15 of Tamuz, the date when Hebrews believe that Aaron built the idol of the golden calf at the foot of the Mountain of God while Moses received the Ten Commandments. So, will the 7th of July be a date when government will attempt to force some sort of false religion upon the people? And, if so, then <u>will there be some traumatic event before that to convince the people of their "need" for some new, government-sponsored religion</u>?

Buckle your seatbelts.

The conversion to digital television takes place just prior to the anniversary of the founding of the modern State of Israel. We have examined several important dates from the Hebrew calendar, and their corresponding dates on the Gregorian calendar. Are there any other dates that we should examine? Oh, yes!

Part of my military duties involved anti-terrorist planning. I also served on two counter-terrorist teams. (The difference between anti-terrorism and counter-terrorism is that the former is preventive and the latter is reactive. In other words, counter-terrorism starts when anti-terrorism fails.) As part of my decades-long study of the topic (before, during, and after my Air Force career), I've learned that Islamist terrorists link their events to certain key dates. (Exactly one year after the "9-11" attacks, there was a crash of an Air National Guard F-16 on a routine training flight. The crash was caused by an odd setting on an electrical switch that cannot be reached without taking apart the dash panel in the cockpit. If you don't already suspect sabotage, perhaps it might help if I tell you that the ANG unit was the same one to which

President George W. Bush belonged in his youth. And, the attack on Tue, 11 Sep 2001 happened on the 60th anniversary of the groundbreaking to build The Pentagon. Coincidence?)

The upcoming 61st anniversary of the founding of the State of Israel (on the 14th of May 2009) precedes the digital TV conversion. At midnight (Eastern Time in the United States), two days after that anniversary, the crescent moon will peak. That is important to Islamists. Most of the time, they match their terrorist attack plans to anniversaries on the Islamic calendar (which, of course, is lunar). The 16th of June 2009 on the Gregorian calendar corresponds to the 22nd of Jumada t-Tania 1430 on the Islamic calendar.

And, that date, the 22nd of Jumada t-Tania, just happens to be *their* anniversary of the 11 September 2001 attacks!

In this writer's opinion, an attack by Islamist terrorists is very likely on the evening of 16 June 2009. At midnight that night (Eastern Time, USA), the crescent moon will peak. Thus, the peak of the moon will also be the start of the 17th of June. That day, on the American calendar, is the anniversary of the arrival of the Statue of Liberty on a boat from France into NY Harbor.

Oddly, the Islamists recognize Jesus as the Messiah of Israel. (The Arabic word for "Christ" is "*al-Mashiach*".) And, as shown earlier in this book, in Hebrew numerology eight is the number of The Messiah. So, in the minds of the bad guys, attacking the "most Jewish city outside of Israel", on a date with a link to the Jewish Messiah (even if most Jews do not recognize Jesus as the Messiah, the Muslims do), and on a date linked to an event that marks one of the big symbols of the United States, is a "perfect storm" of Islamist symbolism.

Once I made that connection, I then looked up the Islamic anniversary (4th of Ramadan) of the 1993 World Trade Center bombing. (Thanks to the work of investigative author and columnist Jack Cashill for his work in connecting WTC bomber Ramzi Yousef to Flight 800.) That anniversary is coming up on 25 August 2009 -- another high-probability date. (I have intel that indicates reasons for targeting Nashville on that date. If I have this info, then it's likely that an extremely wealthy Islamist civil engineer can also obtain that info.)

By the way, while I was typing this, I calculated another date: the anniversary of the Iraqi Out-of-Country Vote. One of the five US cities that held Iraqi elections was Nashville. The fifth anniversary, on the Islamic calendar, will be 09 December 2009.

Again, here are the 2009 dates to watch for terrorist attacks: 29 April, 16 June, 30 July, 25 August, and the 9th of December.

For those that ask, "Well, what about the other religons of the world?", there is also this. The 17th of June happens to be the anniversary of the arrival in the United States (specifically, New York City) of the Statue of Liberty. Some people believe that the statue is pagan in origin, and that its presence in New York Harbor is a curse upon the United States. If that is true, then this coming June will be significant indeed.

My belief is that The War of Gog and Magog is about to start. The cause for that war is detailed in my separate report "On Wings of Eagles". It will soon be available separately from pro-Israel groups.

4th Edition update section ends here

There is no getting around the fact that all of the signs are in place and all of the actors are in the wings of the stage for The Tribulation.

For the person that is already a true Christian, this is a time for inner joy because the claims of the Bible will be fulfilled before our eyes. If we have been looking up with expectant hope, then our "joy will be full". But, for the person that is not a Christian (even if they have previously *thought* that they were), then this could be a terrifying time.

The one thing that makes the difference between joy and terror is faith in Jesus the Messiah. If you have never accepted that faith; or, if your faith has been weak in the past, now is the time to decide to become a subject of the Prince of Peace and of the King of the Universe. Then, you can have confidence that, no matter what happens in the next seven years, you can spend eternity in joy and peace with Jesus — the true Messiah of Israel.

Amen!

About the author

Tom Kovach lives near Nashville, is a former USAF Blue Beret, and has written for several online publications (see below). In 2006, he published his first book, *Slingshot*. Tom is an inventor, a horse wrangler, a certified paralegal, and a former network talk-show host. He has also run for Congress. To learn more, and to order a copy of *Slingshot*, visit: www.TomKovach.us.

www.ingramcontent.com/pod-product-compliance
Lightning Source LLC
Chambersburg PA
CBHW031630160426
43196CB00006B/360